After a few more minutes of succinct conversation the situation became clear.

"Look Sophie." Chris took me over by the window. "Paranoia is running high and wild among the feminists. Jackie thinks that Kathy is an agent and Gerri is checking Julia's references. We spent the morning accusing each other of being government infiltrators. Now we're breaking for lunch."

"What kind of community response have we gotten?"

"Well, as far as I can tell, no one is calling the office for fear that the phone is tapped. Advertisers are slipping notes under the door though, and then running away."

As we stood there a little slip of paper came floating in through the mail slot. We listened to the patter of army boots running down the hall. I picked it up.

> Dear *Feminist News*, please cancel all accounts for Feminist Exterminating Company and please burn all records that we ever did business with you. Please eat this message.

"Sophie, you know as well as I that without that revenue we'll never be able to put out another issue. Sophie . . . ?"

Chris was looking at the floor. "Sophie, if you don't resign, temporarily of course, you know, a leave of absence, we're all going on permanent vacation."

I looked out the window at the two agents sitting in an old Oldsmobile. I knew I had no choice.

THE SOPHIE HOROWITZ STORY

BY SARAH SCHULMAN

the NAIAD PRESS inc.

1984

Printed in the United States of America
First Edition

Cover design by Susannah L. Kelly

Typesetting by Sandi Stancil

Library of Congress Cataloging in Publication Data

Schulman, Sarah, 1958–
      The Sophie Horowitz story.

      I. Title.
PS3569.C5393S6   1984   813'.54   84-3441
ISBN 0-930044-54-1

ACKNOWLEDGEMENTS

I'd like to acknowledge all of the people who gave me their time and encouragement during the completion of this work. Peg Byron, Robin Epstein, Charlie Schulman, Lydia Pilcher, Susan Seizer, Susan LaVallee, Marie Dagata, Steve Berman, Jaime Horwitz, Beryl Satter, Julia Scher, Shirley Arriker, Maxine Wolfe, Sam, Frederique Delacoste, Danielle Frank, Joan Jubela, Bettina Berch, Deb Sherman, Suzanne Seay, Harriet Hirschorn, Stephanie Skura, Stephanie Doba and Stephanie Roth.

I am especially grateful for the efforts and support of Rebecca Sperling, without whom this work never would have been published and Barbara Barracks, without whom Sophie Horowitz would never have come to life.

ABOUT THE AUTHOR

Sarah Schulman, born in New York City in 1958, has published over seventy articles in feminist, gay and progressive publications. *The Sophie Horowitz Story* is her first novel. Her play ART FAILURES (co-authored with Robin Epstein) opened in New York in December 1983. Sarah is currently at work on a second book, *When We Were Very Young: Radical Jewish Women on the Lower Eastside 1879–1919.* She is a recipient of a 1984–85 Fulbright award in Jewish History to Brussels, Belgium.

For Ethel Stevens

The Sophie Horowitz Story

by Sarah Schulman

CHAPTER ONE

I wanted to feed Lillian something delicious because I knew that's what she was going to feed me. Glancing over the meat and poultry case at Key Food, nothing spoke to the sweetness of that woman. Maybe fresh pears stewed in brandy with orange chocolate sauce. "Mmmm," I sighed out loud. "You too baby," winked the stock boy over by the Campbell's soup. Every other weekend for ten months now, she's been coming down on the Friday night express from Boston to wrap her legs around me.

"WHUL, it's four o'clock. You give us a minute, we'll give you the word."

I glanced at the No Smoking sign and lit a Parliament.

"Taxi strike at midnight. Yanks drop to third place. Germaine Covington arrested in bank robbery. Mayor announces plans for Times Square shopping mall, 'Just like Albany' he predicts. All this and more after a word from Mighty-Fine."

My eyes glazed over. My cheeks flushed. My skin turned cold. My palms began to sweat. *Germaine Covington.* It must be twelve years.

Twelve years ago my grandmother and I sat at the kitchen table breaking the ends off string beans and singing Yiddish songs. Suddenly the sky cracked in a giant crash of sound and power. I thought it was the war come home,

1

but nothing followed that first explosion. For a minute one large silence reverberated through the neighborhood, but it was quickly broken by screams and sirens and street sounds as children rushed to the remnants of a recently opened recruiting station two blocks away. We heard the story on the news that night. The bomb had gone off too soon. All the conspirators were killed. All except one. They showed her picture on TV. Germaine Covington looked out at America and her face has stayed with me all these years.

All these years she's been an integral part of my childhood and adolescence. The backdrop of my teenage crisis was her face plastered on post office walls. Six years on the Ten Most Wanted List. Four years as Public Enemy Number One. Around the dinner table my mother would thank her stars I hadn't been born ten years earlier. "You would have ended up just like that girl, throwing away the best things in life." She never said what those things were.

The story came out. She was from a rich family. "The richest," my grandmother said. Her father was vice-president of American Express. She went to a good small liberal college like other young women of her time and caliber. One day she joined a picket line. The next day, a demonstration. Soon she was throwing bombs and killing people. At least that's what the newspapers said. The years passed and the world changed. Most people forgot about Germaine Covington. But not me.

Later that night Lillian and I were hanging out in the tub eating blintzes with sour cream, sucking on Lowenbrau darks. I watched the beer dribble down her chin.

She's a strong woman with a tight body. Her skin and hair are henna-colored except for a patch of bright orange over her left ear. I never know how I feel about her visually. She's got a particular look that speaks to a particular taste like French cigarettes or a Budweiser. She's ten years older than me and likes to fight.

"I remember Germaine from Ann Arbor, 'sixty-seven, 'sixty-eight," she reminisced. "She was the leader of our cell — The Center City Six. We ran into the cafeteria of Dwight D. Eisenhower Intermediate School sticking our fingers in the kids' food chanting 'something's rumbling.' The line then was that elementary school kids were the revolutionaries of the future. By the time they got to senior high school they were already just like their parents so we had to get them early. We occupied the cafeteria, all women wearing football helmets. Mine said Philadelphia Eagles."

A dollop of sour cream fell into the bathwater. "Later that afternoon when we were in jail, Germaine said we had to be willing to risk getting killed by the police. She said we had to give everything to *the struggle*. We had to *smash monogamy*, we had to *break with our parents*, we had to give up our *white skin privilege* and we had to *fight the pigs*. I was scared. I was young. I took out a pen and started scribbling on this roll of toilet paper about how things were getting too heavy for me. I admitted my fears and doubts. I wasn't sure I wanted to *struggle* for the rest of my life. At first it was really exciting. We were trying so many different things. I felt powerful, turning over the world. But the situation was getting tenser, tighter. I wasn't having any fun, just being heavy. I decided I just didn't agree with a small group of people from New York telling me what to do all the time, telling me how to live."

I glared at her.

"Soph — you know what I mean. I felt they were controlling me. I wasn't making decisions for myself. Three weeks later I was summoned to the revolutionary council. Germaine was standing in front of the room in a leather mini-dress and thigh-high leather boots. Rumor was she'd lifted them from Bergdorf's. She pulled out my roll of toilet paper and flung it across the room where I sat stunned. 'This is for *The New Yorker*.' "

Lillian took a reflective drag off her Marlboro Light.

CHAPTER TWO

Saturday morning the *Feminist News* office was buzzing with activity. When you work sixty hours for ninety dollars you often ask yourself why. Days like this, however, made it all seem glorious and electric. Something very heavy had happened and women were looking to us for an explanation. Calls came in from all over the country and even Paris. They wanted information about Germaine Covington. We had nothing about her on file. Most of us were too young to ever have seen her. We didn't even know if she was a feminist.

"I think it's a clear case of male ejaculatory violence," Chris said. "Just look at the dailies."

The New York Times features her Wanted photo on the front page. According to the article, the robbery had been a very sloppy job. They didn't get much money, just a few ten dollar bills and a handful of papers and microfiche. Then the getaway car ran out of gas. Smelled like a setup to me. Everything was recovered including Germaine, but one other woman was seen fleeing into the shopping mall. The police had put up roadblocks all around White Plains but so far she'd eluded them. What was Germaine doing in a mess like this?

"I think Sophie should take this beat."

"Why me?" My instinct said *no*.

"Face it Sophie, you know more about her than any of us. How many times have I heard you wonder out loud what your life would have been like if you were Germaine Covington? You've always nursed revolutionary fantasies, so I know you'll put your blood and guts into it and write a really good piece."

It's true that I occasionally allow myself to dream of something more romantic than a low-budget women's monthly but I still felt nervous. "I'm so busy already. I'm doing a twelve-part story on women and botany and I have an interview on Tuesday with a group of go-go dancers from New Jersey who want to take over the sex industry. I just don't have time for a new project." My phone rang.

"Soph." It was Lillian. "The police just identified the woman who escaped from the scene of the crime. I heard it on the radio. Her name is Laura Wolfe."

My heart sank. I knew Laura Wolfe. We all knew Laura Wolfe. We've all known her for years as the biggest pain in the ass around. She was part of a group known as Women Against Bad Things. They had some kind of politics which none of us understood. Whatever we did, they didn't like it and usually picketed feminist events with very long leaflets. I'd never dream that she would be involved in something as heavy as a bank robbery. I guess I never really took her very seriously.

On the way home I grabbed an order of fried sauerkraut pirogies to go and copies of all the afternoon editions. There were pictures of Laura and Germaine all over the place. *The New York Post* headline read ANTI-AMERICAN, COMMIE, LEZZIE BLOOD-THIRSTY PIG over a copy of Laura's high school graduation picture. I cleared a place on my desk and tacked her photo to the wall.

CHAPTER THREE

Lillian left at three Monday morning to catch the Nightrider back to Boston. I stayed up working on Laura Wolfe until noon. The girls at the office think I can write any story in fifteen minutes, but this was going to be a tough one. Besides, Lillian's smell on my fingers was becoming a serious distraction. By noon I had the itch and decided to grab a piece of cheesecake at Junior's on Flatbush Avenue. I bought all the papers and hopped on the D train. *The Village Voice* cover story caught my eye. I FUCKED GERMAINE COVINGTON by Seymour Epstein. He didn't mention if she came or not.

Junior's is far, but it's worth the trip. Nothing beats that light lemony cheesecake and those loxa orange walls. The waitress was dressed like the world's last dyke. If there was one lesbian left in the world you'd know it was her. She's the kind that pats your ass every time she passes in the bar. She was giving me the once-over when her eye caught Laura's picture in *The Daily News*.

"That bitch."

"You know her?"

"I know her and I wish I never did know her."

"What time do you get off?" I smelled a scoop.

She glanced at my I LIKE GIRLS lapel pin. "Three."

"I'll have another piece of cheesecake. Cherry."

We walked slowly down De Kalb Avenue. Her name was Fran Marino. She was from Canarsie. A couple of years ago she started working in a sleazy Wall Street restaurant. "You just throw the food down and they leave you a buck. The gimme-a-Coursoisier-and-Coke crowd. Real animals." She lit a joint.

"So I see this other girl working there and I could see right away she was gay, but also she had something different about her. Sort of refined or smart or something like that. Not like the other waitresses. All they talk about is taking ups and giving head. So I started to do her favors, little ones, like refilling her water glasses, condensing her ketchups. She was always behind, a terrible waitress. I really covered her ass, even cleaned her ashtrays. We started getting it on once in a while."

The joint was played. She ran her fingers nervously through her butch cut. "One night we were coming out of the movies, this Cuban flick. She picked it. I didn't understand a thing. So we're walking along and she turns to me and says, 'I went to a movie with you, now you have to go to an educational with me.' That was the beginning of the end."

We got into her red Rabbit. She shouted over the radio as we sped across the Brooklyn Bridge. "From then on, every time we did anything normal, I had to go to an educational. The next thing I knew they had me standing on street corners selling their paper *The Young Sectarian*. Then it wasn't good enough that I went to their meetings. I had to bring my friends to their meetings. Then they told me I wasn't going to enough meetings. Then, every time they saw me they told me what I was doing wrong. I shouldn't play ball. I shouldn't go to the bars, except to *organize*. I shouldn't see my friends. I wasn't getting much out of it either. Laura made me do a whole song and dance just to get a little feel."

We turned off the bridge and drove up through the Lower Eastside. I thought about stopping off at the Garden Cafeteria for a little borscht all-the-way. They do a great job with chopped up cucumber, radishes and fresh dill, a hard boiled egg and a boiled potato. By the time I thought twice, we'd pulled up to the Dutchess.

"So one day," Fran continued, "they were having another one of their piddly shit demonstrations where no one goes but them. I finally put my foot down and told her I wasn't going to go."

She ordered a Seven and Seven at the bar. The bartender sneered at me. Her name was Barbie. More than once she had threatened to punch my teeth in for handing out leaflets in that joint. Lesbian liberation and the mafia mix like scotch and prune juice. You don't try it if you don't have to.

"So you know what she had the balls to say to me, that bitch? She turns to me and says 'Sister, I care about you, but if you do not march, we are through. Sister, you are unprincipled.' If the fucking FBI ever came to my door, I'd tell them everything. I hope she fries."

That was my cue to go. You never know who's listening to your conversations. I understood why Fran was pissed off but I hoped she'd change her mind about the FBI. It just wasn't right.

"Look Fran, here's my name and address. If the FBI comes knocking at your door, call me. Don't tell them anything before you call me. They're not nice. They're no good, you know, they're like cops."

"What's wrong with cops, my brother's a cop."

Even my grandmother knows what's wrong with cops. I know they're just little working-class guys who want to have somebody to push around but they're not my friends. This Fran Marino could be trouble.

I walked home along Eighth Street back to the East

Village. This street and I have gone through so much together. It used to be a quiet place when I was little. My
family would go out for Chinese food on Sundays. Now
music blares from the cheap clothing stores run by Sephardic
Israelis. Grease smells emanate from fast food pizza, hot
dogs, Orange Julius and croissants.

So, Laura Wolfe uses sex as a tease to recruit for her
group. Funny, I thought it would be more important to her
than that. Maybe she has real lovers and then she has recruits
who she keeps hungrily salivating on street corners selling
newspapers hoping that if they're good they'll get a little
piece. Even if she's not a good waitress, she's got a strong
will. I'd like to know more about this Laura Wolfe.

CHAPTER FOUR

"Where the fuck am I?"

The streets were empty of people and full of boxes and scraps of polyester. By day the neighborhood bustled with Chinese and Latina women working the sweatshops for ninety dollars a week. Same salary as *Feminist News* but a whole different ballgame. At five o'clock they start smashing into the subways heading for Elmhurst Queens, shopping bags full of take-home sewing, paid for by the piece. Just like grandma used to do. At night the area is deserted except for a few lockouts from the men's shelter huddling around a burning garbage can.

There were two greasers coming towards me in leather jackets and Mohawk haircuts.

Shit, I thought.

I was about to jump into my karate stance when it occurred to me that they were females. This was the place. The Dinette Sette, a new nightspot featuring ambisexual rock and roll. Melonie was appearing there with her new band.

Melonie Chaing was an old acquaintance. It never got to be more than that. When we first met, she was a psychologist at Payne-Whitney married to a psychiatrist at Bellevue and living on the Upper Westside. She walked out of her marriage and her career on the same day. First she went to

Hong Kong, spending her nights walking the streets talking to prostitutes and taking their pictures. She published a photo-essay with a new age press. They called it *Nationalist Cunt: Cash, Charge or Check.* Then she came back to New York and started playing the electric guitar. When the punk scene opened up, Melonie jumped right in, dyed her long hair green and started to "develop an electric Asian aesthetic." She moved back to Chinatown, converting an old sweat shop into a luxurious loft. It was about two blocks from where she grew up. "I've forgotten about my genitals for thirty years," she told her stunned family. And now she just wanted to have fun and carry on in the tradition of the "great and powerful dragon lady." She tours with her band, The Dogmatics. There was a message on my tape that she had some information.

I looked for a corner to squeeze into but the whole place was the size of a corner. It was two bucks for a Schlitz. I smiled at the waitress and leaned against the back wall. The first act, Charlie and the Lesbians, featured a sixteen-year-old boy in a paisley tuxedo with a back-up band of three bulldykes in overalls. They did a reggae version of *Youngblood.* Five or six bands followed that one, all mushing into one endless pink and green sound-check except for this girl group called Beverly Hell and the Five Towns. The drummer could have been a drag queen but I especially liked Beverly with black lipstick on her teeth. It was different. They did sort of a samba rendition of Bei Mir Bis Du Shayn. The Dogmatics came on around four and played a fifteen-minute set. They did ten songs including their underground hits *Jenny Was a Fag Hag* and *Looking for a Chinese Dyke.*

> "I'm looking for a Chinese Dyke.
> I'm looking for a Chinese Dyke.
> I went to a Black bar
> They told me I was white.

I went to a white club
They told me to do outreach.
I'm going home to cry in my tea
Yeah, yeah, yeah."

Melonie wore Saran Wrap, a dog collar and leather cut-outs. As the band reached a rock and roll crescendo, she ran into the audience and emptied out a large mailbag full of Chinese Restaurant take-out menus. In the flashing red light, she set them on fire and doused the flame with Dr. Pepper.

After the show, Melonie told me what I wanted to hear. "I know a woman who has information. Her name is Vivian Beck. We were once in the same place. She knows Laura and Germaine from way back. At least she knew them then. When this whole robbery exploded, Vivian called up the old comrades from ten years ago to organize a response from the academic community. Poor girl, I'm not very academic any more, thank God. Anyway, she's very concerned, and since I heard you were investigating this story, I thought you'd like to talk with her."

Melonie laid out her coke lines like a pro. Now that her ex-husband had finally come out as a faggot, he wrote her prescriptions for pharmaceutical cocaine. The best. At only fourteen dollars a gram, she could re-sell it for two hundred and keep herself in leather.

"Vivian's sort of a lost soul but a good woman. She teaches Italian. Her thesis was on the gourmet cooking utensils of the Italian bourgeoisie. Did you see her book *Knife and Fork as Metaphor*? Here's her number."

I almost asked Melonie for her number. I took another look at the studded dog collar. No, I like adventure in my relationships but only if it's my adventure.

"Thanks pal, see you later."

"Hey Sophie." She grinned. "Keep on rocking."

"Yeah."

CHAPTER FIVE

Vivian wanted to meet at the Prince Street Bar. Being compulsively early I had already cruised all the bookstores and bakeries in the area and still had fifteen minutes. A beer was out of the question. Probably costs three-fifty. Soho is the worst New York City has to offer. Built in a chic shopping-mall motif, its inhabitants resemble victims of the body snatchers, pod people with a vague voidoid quality. A chill ran through my spine. This was really dangerous territory.

I spotted Vivian by the bar. I recognized her by her earrings in the shape of miniature serving spoons. She had so many strange and expensive looking trinkets, sashes, necklaces and bracelets, that she closely resembled a tie rack. Anyone who pays that much attention to detail spent an hour getting ready, which means they had an hour and decided to spend it getting ready. Scary business. Still, on closer examination, I sensed that somehow her heart wasn't in it. The makeup on her face was applied by habit, not passion, and sat on her features like a fly.

"Laura was my roommate and my best friend from 'sixty-five to 'sixty-nine at Sarah Lawrence. I know it's a classically bourgeois place to have gone to school but I didn't have much choice. I grew up in Connecticut after all. My father worked for Nabisco."

Her serving spoons tinkled as she talked. "We had a great time together. I was an Italian major, comp lit minor, I always knew what I wanted to study. But Laura, first it was psychology, then philosophy, then history, then political science, she couldn't get focused. She was always flunking everything and I ended up writing most of her papers for her. We smoked cigars in our room and went to bars with fake ID's and planned on going to Florida over winter break. Then I took a year abroad and Laura spent that time in a new program where college students went into the city to tutor ghetto kids. When I came back she was all excited about some books she had read and new people she met at Columbia. We got into politics together, formed one of the first consciousness-raising groups and read Mao together. We shared our money and our secrets."

Vivian's mauve lipstick stained the cigarette. It burned next to her lipstick-stained glass. Tanqueray and tonic.

"What brand are you smoking, Vivian?"

"Marlboro Light. I don't even have to ask. They just look me in the eye and know that I smoke Marlboro Light. Spacey but smart, a little worried about growing older. Not ready to quit smoking yet though."

I slipped one out of her pack.

"Laura knew the rhetoric better than I did but we were both overcome with the feeling of the moment. Every day was a revelation, not only about how little of what we knew was worth anything, but also that none of us were prepared in any of the important ways to be anyone purposeful in this world. Sometimes the insights gave you elation and power, other times they turned your stomach. I remember one day sitting with Laura over a tunafish sandwich realizing that every bite we took, every cigarette we smoked, every step we made was off the backs of most of the people in the world. It could make you lose your mind. It could also keep you glued to your chair."

"Sort of a *Naked Lunch*?"

"What?"

"Never mind." Vivian felt so familiar, like every character in every Marge Piercy novel.

"My boyfriend, Jerry Silverman, was a big shot in SDS at the time. He was rising into leadership and editing a newspaper out of a communal apartment on the Upper Westside. He didn't like Laura and encouraged me to get away from her and move into his place. There were always nameless, faceless people coming through. It was never clean, there was never any food in the refrigerator. There were always discussions and loud fights and secret plans and people fucking on the living room floor."

"What about you?"

"Oh I fucked Jerry and sometimes he'd tell me to fuck some guy who was getting alienated from SDS."

"Sounds pretty alienating."

Vivian fit in here. Other women were dressed like her and holding their cigarettes in the same way but I could also see her with long straight hair and jeans and her old man's army jacket, ink all over her hands, putting out Jerry's newspaper.

"Then of course, I got pregnant and went home to Connecticut where my parents paid for the abortion. My sister had just married a young man from Nabisco and was about to move down to Westchester. I gave her a copy of *The Politics of Experience*. We had nothing to say to each other. When I came back Laura was busy working in groups that were woman-only. We decided to officially withdraw from school and moved in together to a woman-only communal apartment, also on the Upper Westside. We spent a lot of time together. Even slept in the same bed. I started fucking Jerry again, got pregnant again and married him."

Vivian talked so fast. Like someone who would tell you anything if you only asked. "Then she came out of the hospital."

"When was that?"

"I think it was around nineteen sixty-nine. It was awful. When Laura signed her trust fund away to the Black Panther Party, her parents were very upset. They owned some non-union company in New Jersey that made artificial lawns for stadiums and indoor swimming pools. So that's when they finally interceded. They committed her and put her through electric shock and aversion therapy."

She gulped down the rest of her drink. A little piece of lime was caught between her teeth. "Just like in *Clockwork Orange*. They gave her drugs that put her in convulsions, and showed her pictures of women making love. It was a very expensive private clinic off in the woods somewhere. When she came out she was never the same again. She never had friends after that and believe me I tried. Only her comrades were important to her. The rest of us were simply *unprincipled*."

"Did you try to talk to her about what had happened?"

"I did try Sophie, I did, but I had my own life too. I miscarried. The whole thing miscarried. The revolution wasn't around the corner anymore. I had to go on with my life. I finished my BA at City College and by 'seventy-three I decided to go on to graduate school. I divorced Jerry and I moved to Philadelphia to get my MA in Italian."

"Did you try to contact Laura again?"

"I thought about her every once in a while. When I got married again I tried to contact her. I left a message but she never got back to me."

I was getting hungry. Glanced at the menu. Forget it. "Vivian, do you think she felt let down by her friends?"

"If she did, she never said so. She told each of us about her experience in the hospital and then she never mentioned it again. There were no personal accusations or recriminations. Everything was politics. Either you were *principled* or *unprincipled*. It didn't matter if you wet your bed, talked to the dead, only ate jello on Sundays. As long as you could

regurgitate the political line, well, that was all that mattered."
Tears welled up in Vivian's eyes but she must have been wear-drip-proof mascara because nothing ran down her cheeks.

"Vivian, I know this must be painful for you but please, try and remember what her politics were. I don't really understand it. Were they feminist? Marxist? Can you put your finger on it, so to speak?"

"She called it the theory of the big lie. It was based on the idea that everyone lies to themselves and abuses others to justify their lies. The goal of the revolution is to cut through that. Like the etymology of the word radical is, to get to the root. They called themselves Women of the Roots. At least that's what they called themselves in 'seventy-one. There's been a million splits and new formations since then."

I speared an olive out of the bartender's setup and munched thoughtfully. "What kind of women did Laura work with?"

"A lot of them had been friends of ours at one time or another. But when most of us started readjusting our lives to match a different reality, going back to school, raising families, these women kept at it. They kept at the tiny demonstrations, the long, boring leaflets, educational after educational. They were afraid to go on with their lives."

She paused. "Or maybe we were afraid not to."

Her candor surprised me and it showed.

"I know what you're thinking, Sophie. That all the conditions in the world that motivated our commitments to change were still just as pressing, only our commitments changed. It's true. Most of the women in her group didn't have the same choices I did. They didn't do well by New Left standards. You know, a woman's power depended on the man she slept with. It was a sexist but historically consistent practice. Not that fucking Jerry actually ever did me any good."

Having finished off the olives I started in on the onions.

"Their politics," continued Vivian, "last I understood, went something like this. They argued that if you really want a better world then every institution has to be thrown out or re-evaluated. We have to restructure all of the ways that we relate to each other."

"I'm with you so far."

"If you really want a new culture and a new system, you have to be willing to fight for it. Your personal desire to fit in, in case the revolution doesn't happen, is precisely what keeps it from happening."

"Vivian, it's intriguing. You're so clear about what you do and how you feel about it, and at the same time you accept it as given and unchanging."

Vivian looked at her third Tanqueray. Straight this time. "Look, I know that on some level Laura's right. I've always known it. But I just don't want to live that way. I'm happy with my life and I wouldn't want to change it. I've finally found a man that I don't have any illusions about. He's not what I imagined when I was twenty, but after a few reality checks I realized that just as I'm not living in the world I'd like to be living in, I'm not going to find the ideal man either. It's just not going to happen that way. Anyhow, I'm thirty-four years old now. I can't get up at four in the morning and leaflet factories. I won't stand on street corners talking to people who don't care or don't even know where they are. I don't want to end up like little old ladies from the Communist Party who are still trying to get winos to buy copies of *The Daily World*, and won't accept that their dream has crashed. But I do know one thing. When change finally comes, and it will come, history will remember Germaine Covington and Laura Wolfe as the real revolutionaries. And I hope the day comes when I can tell Laura that to her face."

The bar was filling up. Vivian staggered out the door. I

watched her slide into a cab. I was getting to know Laura Wolfe very well.

CHAPTER SIX

I sat in my apartment. Just sat. The public radio station was droning on and on, a marathon fundraiser. *"Please give us money. Please give us money. Please, please, please."*

The new *Village Voice*, covered in cherry babka crumbs, lay limply in my lap. Seymour Epstein had a first page exclusive interview with Germaine Covington from inside Metropolitan Correctional Center. I reread the story for the third time:

> Sunlight streaming through a slit in the wall illuminated the courageous features of Germaine Covington. Her strong and slightly greying temples. Her sharp jaw. She pointed to a stack of books. "I've been reading Fidel," she said, her clear eyes blazing with revolutionary fervor.

How the fuck did such a fat slob, fake intellectual dog like Seymour Epstein get that interveiw? Where was I? The doorbell rang.

"It's Henry." The voice came up through the intercom.

Henry Tsang was Melonie Chaing's ex-husband. We'd had a brief affair before either of us decided to be gay full time and it was pleasant. We murmured "You're not like all the others" and it didn't take long to figure out that we were right. Henry's real different from Melonie. Comes from a rich family in the burbs. His father's a Chinese scientist and his mother's a Lithuanian refugee from Communism. He was a regular suburban kid, played ball, marched in the high school band and went to medical school just like his parents told him to. But during his first year at Mount Sinai the world started to change and Henry took a leave of absence to find out what it was all about. He began reading those dangerous Chinese Communists he'd heard maligned around the dinner table. Henry joined a pro-China group and firmly believed that in order to organize the workers, he had to live like the workers. The group he belonged to, The February Twentieth League, claimed that workers had short hair, didn't smoke dope, ate white bread with creamy peanut butter. They also lived in stable, monogamous, heterosexual marriages and didn't have oral sex. He tried to be more of a man for the revolution but he always remained lithe and slight, almost like a fairy. Then China began to change and so did his wife. The League split into those who supported Mao and the Gang of Four and those who went with the new China and their neo-capitalist ways.

Henry got depressed and stopped going to meetings. He started working harder at the hospital and reading jogging magazines. Sometimes after work he would go down to the West Village and have a man suck him off in the bathroom. He didn't really think about it when he wasn't doing it and wasn't really sure later that it was him at all. When Melonie left him he was relieved and didn't take it as a personal affront, which it wasn't. Soon he fell in love with Harold, the piano player at Marie's Crisis Piano Bar and moved into his apartment in Chelsea. Henry realized that Melonie was smarter than he and that he had deceived them both in their early years together. Now he didn't understand why she needed to do what she needed to do but he had faith in its value and did his part when told to.

"Henry, you look great," I said. "Sit down, have some food. I've got bagels, smoked herring, schmaltz herring or herring in cream sauce. How's Harold?"

"Soph, listen, I came here to tell you something important."

His eyes caught the walls of my apartment. They were covered from floor to ceiling with pictures, clippings, leaflets and posters depicting Laura and Germaine. Notes overflowed onto the floor. "That's what I want to talk to you about."

He leaned forward on his skinny hips and wiggled his moustache. "I've been on rotation at Bellevue emergency, psychiatric emergency that is, you know, supervising interns so that the experience doesn't make them throw away medicine for a more sane business like . . ."

"Investigative reporting?"

"I don't know." Henry has always been absentminded. "Last night, around four-thirty in the morning, they brought in an important prisoner from MCC. I knew something big was happening because the Westchester D.A. was right there with her."

"Her?"

"Yeah, a woman in very bad shape. She was having a violent psychotic episode, but if you ask me, they encouraged it. She was screaming at the top of her lungs and attacking all the orderlies and doctors. They put her in handcuffs, leg irons, waist chains and a straightjacket."

"Sounds like you guys weren't kidding around. What was she saying?"

"I don't know. She wasn't speaking English — or Chinese for that matter. It was some kind of Mediterranean language like Greek or maybe Armenian, but that's just a guess. Anyway, one thing I do know is you don't take a foreigner who's that upset and wrap them up in restraints. It's ridiculous. It's like asking someone to crack up, they used such poor judgment."

"They?"

"Yeah, the Westchester D.A. was there bossing everyone around. He insisted we shoot her full of Thorazine. A lot of Thorazine. Enough to sedate the Dogmatics and all their friends."

He took a gulp of Dr. Brown's Cel-Ray tonic. "So, I looked at her record. Sophie, guess what her name was."

"Frances Farmer."

"Germaine Covington."

"What?" Inside, my heart skipped three beats. A scoop. I got a scoop. Oh God, please give me this, I'll never ask for anything again.

"Soph, it wasn't her. No way. I haven't seen Germaine since my days with The Yellow Panthers, but still, there is no way on earth this woman was Germaine Covington. That's why I came to see you, Soph. Whoever she was, she was old and had scabs, ulcerated legs. She looked like someone who'd been having a hard time for a long time. I've been thinking it over pretty carefully. You know, I'm not a very impetuous guy, but really, don't you think it's possible that the government got her?"

"Who?" I was thinking about my Pulitzer.

"Germaine. It sounds to me like they're hiding her somewhere and maybe torturing her or who knows what — you know, to get information."

Henry's theory had a high probability rate. The government was known for pulling neat tricks like that.

"Henry, they may have been able to kill Allende but they can't pawn off a Cypriot bag lady as Germaine Covington."

"They can if she's in a box."

"No entiendo."

"She never made it out of emergency. They shot her so

full of Thorazine she choked on her own vomit. I was really worried but the D.A. didn't care. He said he took full responsibility."

"Henry, what do you know about Seymour Epstein?"

"Well, I don't know him personally but he doesn't have a very good reputation on the grapevine. He writes pieces for liberal publications about what a stud he is with the ladies and then at night he cruises heavy men's bars like the Mine Shaft."

"My mind was racing. If only I could get it together, solve the puzzle, publish the story, sell the film rights and have a bestseller before the rent comes due. Only one person held the key.

"I've got to find Laura Wolfe."

CHAPTER SEVEN

Friday night I sat waiting for Lillian to come in off the 6:30 Colonial. The place was a disaster. Cartons of fruit soup and an empty bottle of Krakus beer sat in the bathtub. Everywhere there were packs and packs of cigarettes: Newports, Marlboros, Drum (roll your own), and rolling papers. I even had Pall Malls for those really difficult moments. Copies of the day's *Times, Post* and *News* were spread out on the floor. There was a knock at the door.

"Come in," I yelled but nothing happened.

Ten minutes later another knock. I opened the door to a tall young boy. About six feet tall in a little kid's striped T-shirt and torn jeans. He had glasses that looked like his mother picked them out — large black frames held together by a band-aid, and straight brown hair cut into bangs. On closer examination I realized he was older than his appearance suggested, much older. His full yet clean-shaven beard indicated middle to late twenties.

"Yes?"

"Uh." He rocked back and forth on his pro-keds pulling out the hairs in the middle of his head. Obviously an unfortunate habit. "I'm a friend of Rita's."

"Who?" I asked blankly, trying to decide if it was worth being polite.

"Rita from Missoula."

"Oh." Then I realized I was in trouble. Two years ago my old girlfriend and I had decided to hitchhike cross-country. Being city girls we didn't realize that you just don't hitchhike through Montana in the winter. We never thought it would take us so goddamn long to get from one town to another. Rita found us half-frozen between Billings and Butte and took us to her place in Missoula. It's a small town with a large lesbian underground. We stayed there a week. She was so wonderful, I promised her that if she ever had any friends passing through New York, I would be glad to . . . oh, well.

"Actually, I'm not her friend. I'm her brother."

"Oh well, come in."

That's how Evan came to my house. The beginning was quite simple in comparison with the end. He took up residence in the corner of the kitchen and laid in for the long haul.

"What are your plans, Evan?"

"Well, I'm not sure exactly but I'm sure I won't have any problems. I started college when I was fifteen you know, the University of Chicago. I was sort of a child prodigy."

"How old are you now?"

"Twenty-six."

"So why are you here in New York?"

"I'm going to make it in music. I play the guitar and write my own songs. They're pretty good. Here's one."

Before I learned to refuse, Evan sang at the top of his nose:

> "With blood dripping out of the mouth of the vultures
> The lightning and fire destroying all cultures
> He stabbed her and mauled her and threw her in the creek
> And hitchhiked to Reno and got high with some Greeks."

He looked at me sheepishly. I was beginning to understand that that was his only expression.

"Nice cadence."

He rocked back and forth, pulling out hairs again. "Do you have any food?"

I watched him wreak havoc in my refrigerator, in a way I never thought possible.

"Don't you have any white bread? I only like white bread."

He made himself a dinner of instant coffee and looked very unhappy. "Don't you have any meat? I need meat."

"There's vegetables. They're nice."

"I don't like vegetables, I only like meat. How about rice. White rice?"

He ate some white rice with margarine, not butter, and curled up in a corner with a copy of Hunter S. Thompson's *Fear and Loathing in Las Vegas.*

This was going to be a long, hard winter.

CHAPTER EIGHT

An hour later Lillian walked in.

"Soph." She came and sat on my lap, bringing me into her beautiful softness.

"Hi gorgeous, I'm having a terrible life."

"I saw the papers. I'm sorry."

"Yeah."

"Sophie, you know you deserved that interview. You're a better and more delicious journalist than Epstein any day."

"Thanks Lil, but we've got new problems now."

I showed her the headlines: COP KILLER OD'S IN JAIL HOUSE ORGY.

We stood in quiet reverence for a minute. I filled her in. Then she filled me in. An hour later I was relaxing in the tub sucking on a Guiness Stout while Lily talked to Evan in the kitchen.

"Who's the boy scout?"

"Evan's staying here for a while. Uptight, isn't he?"

"His personality reminds me of a fourth grader with a perpetual hard-on. Sophie, you're awful, always feeling sorry for losers. No matter what you say, I know your mother did a good job on you."

"Now don't go blaming everything on Mom."

She smiled her big smile at me. Lillian has big teeth. She says that one of them is false but I don't know which one.

"Lil?"

"Hmmm?"

"Why do you taste so good? Why do you feel so good? Why are you so exciting, adventurous, aggressive and satisfying?"

"Skin texture," she said, almost absentmindedly.

"What do you mean by that?"

"Skin texture is the key to good old-fashioned, unromantic but sufficiently affectionate, nitty-gritty sex for pleasure. Some people, you like the way they look. You like the way they smell. But when you get next to them, something just doesn't feel right. You know, you can't get comfortable, like it doesn't fit. The key is skin texture and honey, you've got it."

"So that's the key?"

Sometimes I wonder what Lillian sees when she looks at me. I put out my usual old gruff, tough, smooth-operator image and she keeps giving me puppets and underwear with strawberries on them. She's just invented a Sophie Horowitz who is vulnerable and childlike and that's who she relates to. No, not all the time, sometimes she likes me to be strong and sweet.

"Yes Soph, Seymour Epstein is definitely the key." She rubbed her toe on my pubic hair. "He made up this interview, that much is clear. So now Germaine is dead, not the real Germaine but some poor Mediterranean bum or revolutionary or whatever she is. While our heroine sits in the clutches of the FBI, we sit in a sagging tenement knowing that Seymour is, undoubtedly, the key."

Lillian is so smart. Sometimes I feel like suggesting that she give up her nice boring, fair-paying job in Boston and get into the swing of things down here. But I know she's not that way. She likes to have her cake and eat it too, and I'm dessert, so to speak. Besides, I wouldn't be happy with a girlfriend I could see every day. I know that much from

experience. After enough years of good starts and bad end-
ings I've learned that a weekend lover and confidante is the
most I would ever want. Well, maybe three days by the beach
thrown in for romance's sake, but that's it.

"Sophie, you know you're really special."

"No I'm not, I'm really not. You just think I am, that's
all."

"Well, maybe not special, maybe unique is more like it."

"Look Lillian, I admit I'm not exactly what you'd call
run of the mill but don't get carried away. I'm typical of a
kind of person who just doesn't get much publicity, so it
looks like I'm special. Anyway, listen, here's what I found
out about Seymour. He's egotistical, a braggart, fat and disgusting."

"Fat people are not disgusting." Lillian is a former
member of the Fat Dykes Liberation skinny support group.

"True, but he happens to be both those things. Plus,
he's a closet case and a masochist, you know, a bottom.
He cruises fuck bars, gets fucked up and then he gets
fucked." I swam over to Lillian's side of the tub and put
my arms around her neck. She thoughtfully ran her fingers
down the crack in my ass.

"Sophie, I think I've got an idea."

CHAPTER NINE

I was thankful for the cool October air. Lillian and I sat in Chris' cab chain-smoking Camel straights. Chris let us use it on the condition that I put in extra hours pasting up the newspaper this month. The wind cooled the sweat on my forehead but not the rest that slowly dripped over my body from a combination of leather and fear.

I have to admit we did look kind of cool. Lillian dressed as a cabby with a newsboy hat and a big cigar. Her henna'd hair tucked away with bobby pins. She's a big woman with strong muscles. I like that.

I glanced at myself in the rearview mirror. "Lil, you know, I don't think Melonie believed me when I told her I needed her leather getup for a story. She had that look in her eye like 'Sure Soph, your girlfriend comes into town and the next thing I know you're sauntering around in here wanting to borrow a leather jacket and pants for work.' "

"Well, I wouldn't believe you either. Are you sure you're not getting some kind of thrill from wearing those clothes? I'm getting one from watching you."

The leather was strong and soft. Like Lillian. It was good protection. "I'm glad you're here Lily, it makes me feel safer."

"My pleasure."

"That haircut is a little too butch for me, though, don't

31

you think?" I examined my clone cut. Between the clothes, hair, fake beard and padded crotch, I was convincing if not ravishing.

"Don't worry Sophie, I know the real you. Butch in the streets, femme in the sheets."

The radio played Sarah Vaughn singing *Stairway to the Stars*. We were quiet for a moment, letting her take us along.

It was 2:30 on a Saturday night. We parked outside Epstein's apartment on Central Park West and 95th Street, number 350. It had been an hour since I called his number asking for Beverly Hell. She really stuck in my mind. So, we knew he was home and hoped he wouldn't spend his Saturday night in front of the TV. Even though it probably was cable. We'd been waiting since eleven swapping stories, singing songs. I kept readjusting the lump of foam rubber between my legs until Lillian volunteered a blow job. I took a rain check.

Just then Seymour stepped out into the night. He was smiling, in full leather, cap and all. We followed his taxi down Broadway. The city was completely alive, the way it looks from an airplane coming into Kennedy airport on a summer night. A one-celled organism. A paramecium with fluorescent protoplasm.

He got out at Sheridan Square. As usual the streets were packed with gay people and the cafes were packed with straights. He stopped in at Ty's for a drink. It's a nice place — flannel shirts. People know each other and come to meet their friends. I noticed Seymour ordered a Jack Daniels. That was the first good thing I could say about him.

We followed west along Christopher Street. Me on foot and Lillian behind the wheel. Then it was Boots and Saddles. After that, Christophers. Each time I followed him into a bar, he'd order a shot of Jack. Seymour never tried to connect with any of the men. Not even a smile. He

just watched and so did I. Most of them were really beautiful. Thin and tan, well dressed. They laughed and smoked
and talked with each other. Sometimes in the corner there'd
be a guy dressed in cowboy clothes just holding on to his
beer and staring out from behind his large moustache. But
most of these men were friendly and relaxed. It's funny, but
it occurred to me that none of the straight men I'd ever
hung out with were so good-looking. They certainly didn't
know how to talk to other men, except about avant garde
jazz or Jack Kerouac. Faggots aren't bad really. They know
how to have a nice time and I bet every man in that bar could
iron his own shirts.

By the time we crossed Hudson Street Seymour must
have been a little tipsy. Then I realized that the scenery was
changing. No more nice little cutesy bars. There seemed to
be more street action. Some young Puerto Rican boys were
hanging out by the entrance to the PATH train. A few had
pink and yellow streaks in their feathered hair. I watched an
all-American blond type cruise a Black transvestite prostitute
from his Toyota with New Jersey plates. She wouldn't have
a thing to do with him. I've always admired drag queens —
they have style and courage, and they're very tough. After
all, it was drag queens, Black drag queens, who fought the
police at the famous Stonewall Inn rebellion in 1969. Years
later, a group of nouveau-respectable gays tried to construct
a memorial to Stonewall in the park across from the old
bar. The piece consisted of two white clone-like thin gay
men and two white, young lesbians with perfect noses. They
were made of a plaster-like substance, pasty and white as
the people who paid for it. Some of us were furious. Chris
called together all of the black gay and lesbian groups in the
city and *Feminist News* got involved in the fight for a full
color statue of a black drag queen throwing a brick at a cop.
We didn't get it, and frankly, I'd rather have nothing. At least
that way you know what you've got.

I recognized one of the queens, my neighbor Rick. He was a nice guy, always lending me stockings, dresses and heels when I needed to infiltrate right-wing conferences or go to court. I didn't want to let him spot me. He'd feel bad that I left him out of the fun. Anyway, my instinct said to keep the whole affair hush-hush. It could get sticky.

At West Street I followed Seymour out to the docks. It's a beautiful view of New Jersey at night, all lit up over the Hudson, but I think the men are drawn there by the seclusion and element of danger. There are large holes in the rotting wood and rats openly scamper around the exposed bodies. All around me was the sound of men having orgasms. It was definitely weird, but sort of exciting — you know, different. Men's sex sounds and the smelly breeze from New Jersey. Still Seymour didn't approach anyone. He just stood and watched and smoked a joint and then a cigarette.

Leaving the dock, we headed towards the Ramrod, the famous fuck bar. A few years ago some gay men were hanging out in front, on the street, and a car drove by and opened up with a submachine gun. The killer got off on an insanity plea. Claimed they were trying to make him be a homosexual. Just by standing there. Some people said that if he had shot Wall Street executives, he never would have gotten away with it. Chris says there are plenty of Wall Street executives at the Ramrod. They just wear different clothes.

By this time Seymour was really high. He started a fight with the bouncer about the ten dollar cover. I was glad he did because Lily and I only brought fifteen dollars and I didn't want to start spending it just to get into places. Before it went too far, Seymour cursed out the bouncer and moved up West Street past the leather store, the bikers' bar, past the car cruisers and the trucks, through the meat-packing district. He was looking for something. The sidewalk was covered with blood and the garbage cans overflowed with dead meat parts rotting and filling the air with a nauseating stench. Then he disappeared down a narrow staircase. The sign said ASS*TRICK. A porcelain cast of some man's ass hung over the entry way. Cover was only five dollars, one drink included. I followed him in.

The place was pretty crowded. It had an air of intentional sleaze. All these big men in leather suits, caps, some with whips or spurs. It wasn't scary at all, everything seemed so artificial. Maybe in the early days when leather was starting to get so popular, there was more of a thrill of danger about it. But now, anyone can wear leather. I wondered what the next fad was going to be. Maybe paper? These men were dancers and CPAs and graduate students in Marxist Political Economy. So, they dress like Hell's Angels once in a while, big deal. I'd suspect it would get boring after a few months. I noticed the walls covered with photos, drawings, replicas and representations of penises. Enormous, swollen and grotesque penises, as if they were Betty Grable pinups or other graven images.

"Gross," I said to myself. Clearly, I didn't want to stay there longer than I had to.

I waved to the bartender. "You see that guy over there? When he orders a drink, make it a triple." I put my ten on the bar. Didn't get any change.

By four o'clock the moment had come. Seymour was literally on his knees sliding even further down along the side of the bar. Men was discoing over him. I knew it was time to act. The trick was to keep him away from my fly. Fortunately, Lillian had thought of this in advance. I grabbed his wrists and handcuffed them behind his back.

"Drink," I commanded and poured the triple shot down his throat.

"Come on you little scum, I'm taking you home." I had worried a little about the humiliation part, but it wasn't hard at all. I pushed him into a conveniently waiting cab.

"Tell me more," he drooled.

"You disgusting shit. You don't deserve the leather on your back."

I pulled his cap over his eyes. "Just sit there and don't say a word."

Lillian drove us home. Just as we expected, he was passed out by the time we got there. The doorman was rather large. His nameplate said Mukul Garg. He seemed to be used to Seymour's behavior and pretended not to notice the cuffs. We carried the dead weight up to Seymour's apartment.

I opened the door with Seymour's keys and threw him on the bed. He had a pretty nice place for a sometimes employed free-lance writer. I found a leather mask on his night table and tugged it over his head, leaving the eye and mouth zippers open for air. I knew I didn't have much time. I grabbed whatever a good detective would grab — papers, bills and a little metal box locked to the desk. It was easy to pick. One of the skills I learned from watching television. I noticed a copy of *Feminist News* opened to my article *A Wolfe In Wolf's Clothing.* Chris always picked out the titles.

"Well, what do you know about that." I smiled to myself. It was nice to be noticed, but this wasn't the moment to dwell on it. I dashed out the door leaving Seymour snoring like a baby.

CHAPTER TEN

Sunday we slept till three. First I was groggy and then jubilant. What a coup! We celebrated our success over breakfast. I noticed that Evan had done a little shopping. The fridge was filled with white bread, Kraft macaroni and cheese in a box, cans of corned beef hash and a bottle of ketchup. I felt a little queasy when I noticed the ketchup stains on the mouth of the milk carton.

"Watch out Lil, I think the milk has cooties."

"That boy really is unpleasant, isn't he?"

"Yeah, you know what drives me mad? How he sleeps in his clothes and never changes them and smells bad all the time and walks into a room like he's the only one in it and relates to the world as if nothing happens when he's not there."

"Well, Sophie, you know what happens when you eat all those nitrates and nitrites, it stimulates the testosterone."

We cleaned up the greasy bags and remnants of Chinese take-out and tried to pick up the grains of white rice that had fallen between the floorboards.

"I couldn't believe the expression on Seymour's face when you brought him to the cab," Lillian said between mouthfuls of scrambled egg.

"He looked almost thankful. You know Soph, in a weird way I think we made him happy."

"Well," I replied, slurping some cold cucumber soup, "He's not going to stay happy when we figure out how he's involved in all this. I think we got some good information in those papers we swiped from his desk."

"Sophie, don't they ever eat eggs on the Lower East-side?"

"No, we eat cold cucumber soup," I replied a bit sharply. We'd been through all this before.

Sometimes I don't really understand why Lillian and I get along so well. There have definitely been some rocky moments since we first met.

I gave a talk in Boston at the invitation of a local lesbian group, one of those coalition efforts where people with nothing in common except their opposition to something pretend to work together. They close their eyes temporarily to the fact that if any of them ever got power, they would quickly obliterate the others. After weeks of *struggle* — caucuses, manipulations and purges — they plan a program where each group has one speaker and three minutes to talk about their issue and ignore everybody else: "One of you and one of you and one of you." It's pretty undialectical if you ask me.

On the platform was Mark Wilson, a Marxist economist from the New School for Social Research. He wore a brown corduroy jacket with leather elbow patches. He used indecipherable economistic lingo to talk about the crucial role of intellectuals in the leadership of the working class. The second speaker was Richard Gordon, associate professor of Latin American intellectual and political history at Yale University. He wore a grey corduroy jacket with leather elbow patches and used indecipherable historical and political lingo to talk about the crucial role of intellectuals in the leadership of the working class. I wore my Patti Smith T-shirt with cutoff sleeves and called my talk *Heterosexuality: What Is To Be Done?* There were 400 people in the room. Afterwards there was a three-hour question and answer period. No one asked me a single question. *The Boston Globe* did a short piece on page thirty-six. They spent a paragraph on each of the two gentlemen. The last line said, "Susan Horowitz, a feminist, was angry."

After the talk, a bunch of us went out to a local bar called The Saints. I was tired and cranky and let the chit-chat circle around me like cigarette smoke. Out of boredom I started a bit of girl-watching and noticed that one girl was watching me. Every ten minutes or so we would check in with each other. Our eyes would meet and we would both look away. Hours passed. Finally the place was empty and quiet. I turned down a few rides back to where I was staying and ended up sitting alone with a glass of flat tonic water and an overflowing ashtray. Besides the bartender cleaning up, we were the only ones left in the place. Finally, feeling a bit dizzy, and for drama's sake, I got up to wait outside. Standing in the early morning air, one foot flat against the wall, like the narcs posing as gay men on the cruise in Washington Square Park, I waited. I waited like Humphrey Bogart. I swung my jacket over my shoulder and waited. I smoked a cigarette and waited. Then another. Fifteen more minutes passed but no sign of Madame X. I practiced what I would say. I tried out, "Hi." No, too wimpy. "Are you looking for me?" No, too moronic.

At that moment the door opened and out she walked, on the arm of her girlfriend, the bartender. Oh well. Feeling like a fool I took a cab back to the Cambridge house where I was assigned to sleep. I walked in at four a.m. to the sight of a woman on all fours scrubbing the kitchen floor.

"It's for my nerves," she said. That was Lillian.

She offered me a cup of tea. "Camomille, Red Zinger, Rose Hip, Purple Haze?"

"Don't you have real tea? Like Lipton?"

She did. We sat down together and talked. She was from a small town in Michigan. Her father was a mechanic and her mother sewed for the Woolco chain. She worked hard all through high school to be able to go to college and ended up at the University of Michigan at Ann Arbor in the fall of 1967. All around her, middle- and upper-class kids, kids from New York and California, Jews and Communists and Hippies and even some Blacks, were running around campus changing the world. At least that's what they said. She lived in collective houses and did street theatre, worked the people's clinic and did a radio show called *Free Waves.* But, when the revolution was over, they went back to school and Lillian went back where she came from. She married a local boy and after a year started an affair with a married woman who lived on the same street. They had gone to high school together, although they never hung out with the same crowd. When her old man found out, the two women fled in the middle of the night and hitched on the interstate to New York City. A month later, Lily realized that she was pregnant and knew she had to get an abortion. The two of them scraped together every possible penny and Lillian hitched with truckers down to the famous abortion doctor in Pennsylvania. The story was that he had turned his back on his own daughter when she was pregnant. She died on a kitchen table. From then on, he did as many as he could do with a minimum of contact with the women. He didn't speak with them or look them in the eye. He just took the cash, did the job and left the room. By the time Lillian got back to New York, her girlfriend was gone. She had returned to her husband in Michigan. Lily has called her a few times over the years. It's sort of a tradition. Lily calls and the woman hangs up. Sometimes a child answers, though she's not sure yet if it's a boy or a girl, the voice is so high. After a few months Lillian moved to Boston and started working as a typist for a publishing company. She's been there ever since. Every other weekend she counsels rape victims from the Women's Center Hot Line.

I felt shy around her age and experience. I hoped she'd overlook my lack of sophistication for the thrill of having a young lover full to the brim with cute bravado. That night, wearing a sleeveless T-shirt that showed off her long neck and throat, she looked like someone I wanted to throw my arms around and climb into.

"Let me taste some of that cucumber soup." She smiled. "Well, it's not too bad." That was an apology.

"Oh Lillian . . . Let's take a look at Seymour's papers."

CHAPTER ELEVEN

Evan sat staring into space in the living room. A nickel bag of pot was spread out on a frisbee, seeds on the table, occasionally rolling onto the floor.

"What are you doing?"

"Nothing."

"I don't mean right now, I can see that for myself. What are you planning to do today?"

"Nothing."

"Well, I wish you would do something because I really need to work today at the typewriter after Lillian leaves and in order to do that I need some time in this apartment to myself. You know, I need to sit around for a while and listen to the radio and make coffee and smoke a cigarette and think and write a few pages and then play a record and write some more pages and I can't do that if you're sitting here all day long, Evan."

I tried to smile.

He looked distressed. Maybe I was too harsh.

"Look, why don't you read a book or something. I have a lot of interesting books. Here's one called *For Men Against Sexism*, you'll really like it."

"Don't you have *The Dharma Bums* by Jack Kerouac?"

"No, I do have Alan Ginsberg though."

"No, I don't think I want to read that."

"Evan, why ever not?"

"Well, he's — you know, he writes about those sailors and everything. I mean, I don't care about what a person does in private, but they shouldn't go imposing it on other people."

"He's gay, you mean."

"Yeah, I mean it's really weird here in New York whenever I walk down the street these men are always looking at me and trying to touch me. It's really disgusting. They'd better watch out or one day I'm going to get really mad. That guy in the building. The one that wears women's clothes. He's really gross. The other day he . . . well." He looked at his pro-keds.

"Don't tell me he made a pass at you."

"Yeah."

"What did he do?"

"He showed me a poem and in it there was this guy who was a homosexual."

"And?"

"That's all — I mean I could just tell that he showed it to me because he was coming on to me, you know he was being so nice and everything. It makes me sick."

"That's why you like Kerouac, right? A good macho buddy-buddy, drinking wine and fucking waitresses."

"Yeah, that's America."

"It sure is."

I've known boys like this my whole life. They want to go on the road with Jack and Neil but they can't tie their own shoes.

When Lillian got back with the Sunday *Times* we went into my room and locked the door.

"You know Soph, if I were you, I'd be very concerned about having Evan around all the time. You never know what information he's picking up. I'd be real careful."

"Oh, he's just a pain in the ass but he's harmless. He's

just a jerk, not a troublemaker. Believe me, I'm a very good judge of character. Now let's get to work." But just to be safe I stuffed towels under the door before flipping through the evidence.

"Let's see. Phone bills, rent receipts, bank statements, lots of good detective work here. Bills from Brooks Brothers, Lutece, Pleasure Chest . . ."

"Well, let's look at the phone bill. We can see if he made any weird or consistent long-distance calls. It's a good source for clues."

"Lillian, how do you know these things?"

"I read detective novels on my lunch hour. Three a week."

"The working girl's soap opera."

"Sophie, don't be so snotty. Some of them are really good. They're about all kinds of contemporary issues. There's even a gay detective. There's books about gentrification and capitalism and all that stuff that you like — only it's human, that's why I enjoy it."

We looked at the phone bills. It was a good idea. Seymour apparently called the same number in Elizabeth, New Jersey, every Tuesday at one o'clock in the afternoon. A definite clue. There was also one Westchester number that looked vaguely familiar, but so do all phone numbers.

"Okay Sherlock, what's next?"

"Well, according to King James —"

"Don't tell me, you read the bible on your coffee break."

"No, King James is one of my favorite mystery writers. He wrote about two hundred books. Anyway, his detectives are real professionals. They always know just what to do next. They're smooth and daring."

"Okay, I got the message." Sometimes I was happy that Lillian went home after three days.

"Sophie, why are you on this macho trip of having to be as tough as Spencer Tracy? You act so big with all these unreasonable expectations and then you can't even keep a weak schlep like Evan from walking all over you."

I was getting angry. "I don't want to talk about it."

"Well, I'm not surprised."

I know, all right, I'm bad. I just don't like to talk about things, especially relationships. Other things on the list of topics I don't like to talk about are my character flaws, the workers, psychoanalysis, Sartre, when you did your laundry and what you had for breakfast. Also, haircuts.

Seymour had some bank statements recording a series of deposits. Some were marked with red pen. FUCK YOU PETER POPE YOU ASSHOLE was scribbled in the corner of one. I made a mental note.

"So you think Seymour could have had something against Catholics?"

"I don't know, Sophie, look at this. Seymour got a rejection letter from *Esquire* magazine. 'Dear Mister Epstein, I'm sorry but we have decided that we are unable to offer you an advance to write an article on the White Plains Affair. If you do complete the manuscript be sure to send us a copy. We do want to say that your choice of a title *A Wolfe in Wolf's Clothing* is splended.' "

"That cocksucker."

"Now Sophie."

"Well, can you imagine ripping off my title like that? He must think no one reads *Feminist News*. Well have I got news for him, he happens to be stealing from the Alexander Cockburn of the feminist press. When this is all over I'm going to sue him for everything he's worth: the apartment, his leather jacket . . .' "

"Oh my God."

Lillian was staring at the contents of Seymour's small metal box.

"Well, what is it?"

Silently Lillian lifted out a small plastic bag. It took me

a moment to realize that the fine white powder wasn't laundry detergent. Cocaine, my nose started to run.

Three beautiful ounces of cocaine. So many times in my short life, I've come home from a long day at a boring job, or a long day without a boring job, worrying about money, dreaming of the paper bag lying in the street revealing a treasure of cocaine. Walking home nights from my job at a nursing home, I would fantasize a black car screeching around the corner into the night, bullets flying out the windows, another black car gaining on them. They hit a bump and a small briefcase flies out of the trunk, only they unknowingly speed on through the streets of the dark city. Unsuspectingly I wander over to the suitcase, snap the combination lock and reveal bags and bags of cocaine. Sometimes this fantasy includes cash. Then I have to figure out what to do with it. Knowing that 90 percent of the population of New York City would kill you for that much coke makes me want to get rid of it fast. I settle for one million in cash, a fraction of the street worth and give a big party, turning on winos to ounces of the best pot. "Don't say I never did anything for you," I'd snarl, throwing a bag of sense at some mean criminal type.

"Earth to Sophie."

"Hmmmm?"

"Look Soph, I know it's tempting but I really think we shouldn't touch this now. You just don't know what might happen. I just think we should put it back in this box and wait a while until we're sure everything's okay."

"Or we can snort it now and then everything will be okay."

"Sophie, just in case."

So, unwillingly, I agreed. We shut the box with the lock from my window gates and Lillian took the key. Before we put it away I decided to take one last look and noticed a small coke spoon. It was a souvenir spoon, like the kind you'd buy at the Statue of Liberty. The china bowl was silver rimmed, featuring a hand-painted portrait of the Leaning Tower of Pisa. The handle was made of silver filigree, carefully woven into a tree with small copper figures of frolicking peasants. At the top sat a tiny silver bust of a bald man with his mouth hanging open. Enameled into the porcelain plaque was his name — Galileo.

CHAPTER TWELVE

It was late Monday morning when they found Seymour's body belly up in the Hudson River. The police were shocked by the sight of a three hundred pound man in a leather face mask, leather thong tied tight around his neck, and wrists handcuffed behind his back. His floating body was surrounded by Chlorox bottles tied together with plastic from six-packs. *The New York Post* suspected a BRUTAL SEX CULT. The doorman, Mukul Garg, told *The Post* that Epstein often came home dressed like that. He remembered a young white man in a leather jacket enter with Seymour, stay fifteen minutes, and then run out. The police broke down a locked door in the apartment, uncovering stereos, cuisinarts and other hot items. Seymour was a fence.

I think it would be fair to say that terror ran through my body like traffic on the FDR Drive, and jammed up all my intersections. For the first hour I was in the most severe panic of my middle-class life. First I packed all my books. Then I unpacked everything except my feminist books. Then I repacked everything except for my feminist poetry books, and then I realized that packing and unpacking wasn't going to get me anywhere.

My next response was a desire to call Eva. Eva was my first girlfriend. We were best friends in junior high school and fell in love during the spring of ninth grade. We never ran out of things to say. We sat next to each other in every class, spent the afternoons together drinking Tab and eating Fritos with dip. On weekends we went to movies. *Persona, Cries and Whispers, The Story of Adele H;* we saw ourselves in every lead character, as long as each spoke a different language. Then we would tearfully part at Grand Central as I headed back into Manhattan and she caught the number seven home to Elmhurst. At night, after our parents were asleep, we would hang out on the phone until we collapsed from exhaustion, and then meet the next morning for coffee and to sneak cigarettes. Always Marlboros.

It was the most passionate, lustful, loving, beautiful experience of my life and it was over before I was old enough to vote. The last time we made love was the night of the blackout in New York City. Two years later she got married. The wedding reminded me of a nose job. Eva, headed towards law school, glowing on the arm of Eddie Weinblatt, a recent MBA from Brandeis. The carnations were spray-painted blue and the band played *Windmills of Your Mind* as they walked down the aisle. At the reception I got morbidly drunk and began seeing all the guests as one large angry mob. When we were lovers we had to hide everything, but because he's a man, they get a party. After three whiskey sours I got sick and left before the consomme.

The last time we ran into each other, she was wearing a full-length fox coat. Once, about a year ago, I called her on a whim. Her maid answered and turned out to be an old friend of mine from when we waitressed together at the Brew and Burger.

"Mrs. Weinblatt" was "at the Hamptons."

But all said and done, Eva was the best friend I ever had and whenever I needed a best friend, I needed her. There is a limit, however, to my self-deception. I knew she would not be amused to hear that I was involved in the murder of a leftie journalist with possible mob connections who I had stalked in a gay leather bar dressed as a man with a stuffed crotch. No, calling her just didn't seem to be the right thing to do.

At that moment the phone rang. I knew it had to be the police. I was trapped. There was no way out. They probably had the whole block covered with sharpshooters. At that very moment they might be handing my mother the bullhorn to implore me to surrender. "Sophie, Sophie, can you hear me you *shmendrik*?"

"They'll never take me alive, Ma."

"Sophie, how can you do this to your father and me? We're the laughing stock of the whole neighborhood. Don't give us any more *tsuris*. If you come out like a good girl, with no trouble, maybe if we change our names, no one will remember in ten or twenty years."

I decided I'd better answer the phone — otherwise they might burst in, guns blazing. "Hello."

"Hello, Sophie."

"Yeah."

"This is Vivian Beck. You remember me don't you? We had such a nice talk in Soho the other day."

"Sure Vivian. How are you?"

"I'm fine. How are you?"

"I'm fine, just fine, sitting here, nothing's happening, everything's cool, peaceful, no problems, just a lazy typical afternoon."

"That's nice."

"So, what can I do for you Vivian?"

"Well, I really enjoyed that little talk we had the other day and I think I might have some more memories that could help you with your story. That is if you are still interested."

"Sure."

"So, do you want to get together sometime this week? I thought Thursday might be a good day. In the afternoon?"

"Yeah, that's fine. You teach at Hunter College, don't you?"

"That's right."

"So why don't I meet you under the Marine statue on Fifth Avenue at three?"

"Fine."

"See you then. Nice talking to you, Vivian."

Well, if the cops got me before Thursday, Vivian could read about in *The New York Post*. I sat down on the couch. I knew I should review my life because it was about to be over. Maybe I'd be lucky and get thirty years. With good behavior I'd be out in twenty. Life begins at forty anyway. One thing was sure, I wasn't going to be able to concentrate with Evan in the house. He was playing the record player again. It was so loud the silverware was trembling in the kitchen. Someone should charge the boy with stereo abuse. For hours and hours I would first hear Bob Dylan, then Leonard Cohen, then Phil Ochs, then Neil Young, then Bob Dylan again. Lillian calls it angry young men music. It was the only kind he liked. I was beginning to wonder why I let Evan stay around. It was certainly far beyond the call of duty. But I had to admit that despite his disgusting habits of being, there was one perverse quality about Evan that made me sort of fond of him. We shared the same scope of self-perception. Either we were everything or we were nothing. There were no other possibilities. Anyway, by comparison to Evan, my life felt successful.

"Don't you ever listen to anything else? Here, try this Betty Carter album."

"I don't like jazz."

"How can you say 'I don't like jazz?' What kind of comment is that?"

I taunted, ranted and raved, but little could jar his Midwest stupor. He had come to New York so full of himself and with unreasonable expectations. Now I knew what was happening. It was the same old syndrome, I'd seen it a million times before. New York is a great place to be if you're doing something and the wrong place to be if you're doing nothing. It swallows you whole and you disappear forever into an apartment or a job or a bar. Even if you have the courage and brains and luck to get out, you're never the same again, because you know all your life that you've failed in New York. Evan was lying sprawled at the bottom of the crevice.

"Look Evan, you just sit in this apartment and smoke nickel bags and listen to the same records over and over again. Why are you in New York? What's your purpose here? Okay, so you didn't make it in music. That's not everything. This is the most beautiful place in the world. Go for walks, look at people, explore, open yourself up, take guitar lessons."

"I already know how to play the guitar."

So he continued to sit there rolling another joint from another nickel bag. Sooner or later he had to run out of nickels, then, I guessed, he'd probably go home. In the meantime I needed some air to get my head straight. I put on my black sunglasses and started to walk down Second Avenue through the Lower Eastside.

CHAPTER THIRTEEN

Tears welled up in my eyes as I looked at the familiar buildings. How beautiful they were. Soon I would be gone, underground. My people, will I ever see you again? The cold sweat of fear started to turn into bristles of excitement. I would miss the neighborhood, my friends, the people hanging out on the stoops drinking Colt 45, but I had no choice. If I was to carry on my work, this was the only solution. Better to be free and move with the wind than spend the rest of my life in prison. On the lam. My picture would replace Germaine's on the walls of post offices around the country. Young mothers would whisper to their daughters "There goes a hero." From safe house to safe house, people preparing for my arrival. "Sophie is coming," they would nod knowingly to each other.

The light changed. Wait a minute, asshole, wake up. This is ridiculous. I haven't done anything for anyone. I've just spent my life being a bourgeois feminist. No, no Lone Ranger for me. It would be a solitary life. An anonymous life. Wandering from town to town riding the freights, working on an oil rig here, in a Holiday Inn there. For the rest of my life I would be a woman without a name, a lady without a country, a stranger in a strange land. First I'd hitch to Montreal, a wedding band on my left hand for protection. I'd say my husband is in the service. The truckers would tell me their army stories. Then, I'd hop a tanker for Europe where I would spend the rest of my life under an assumed name. I tried out aliases: Emma Goldman. No, too obvious . . . Emma Goldstein.

As a young girl I had walked these streets with my grandmother on the way to the Yiddish theatre to see *The Dybbuk* or *Yoshe Kalb*. She'd clutch my hand as we rushed past the Fillmore East where barefoot kids in painted faces sat laughing at nothing. Afterwards we'd eat kasha varnishkas at Ratner's Dairy Restaurant where every table got a whole basket of onion and pumpernickel rolls for free. All those memories made me hungry. If I was going to have to go underground I should at least allow myself a little treat. I stopped at the B and H Dairy for a good knish. That was the only place left that didn't microwave. Tears ran down my cheeks dripping into a glass of cold schav with sour cream.

Stumbling home I saw an omen on the marquee of the St. Mark's Theatre. Maria Schneider! A Maria Schneider double feature. What bliss. I would do anything for that woman, anything. I would even sit through two hours of Marlon Brando and two hours of Jack Nicholson for her. Rumor has it on the lesbian grapevine that while she was filming *Last Tango In Paris*, her girlfriend got hysterical at the sex scenes and had a nervous breakdown. Maria, tried and true, moved into the psychiatric hospital to be near her lover, only leaving to go to the set. Well, supposedly it was in *People Magazine*. All right, it may not be exactly true, but it makes a great story.

When the films were over I felt a whole lot clearer. Retracing my steps I found it hard to believe that I would get caught. The only people who really had a good look were Seymour and Mukul Garg. Mukul wasn't a problem. Only Lillian knew the real score, and Melonie thinks I used her toys for some illicit fun. The thing to do was be professional. If I ever wanted to get picked up by one of the big dailies, I would have to make it my business to get some more scoops. Make an underground name for myself. I had to put my petty fears aside, my ego in check and solve this mystery. Who killed Seymour Epstein? Where is Germaine Covington? And what about Laura Wolfe?

CHAPTER FOURTEEN

Tuesday morning I woke up to the sound of typing from across the alley. It had started about three weeks before. I guessed another writer had moved onto the block and I felt a warm comaraderie. Some mornings we'd be typing duets, our different rhythms coming together in a symphony of productivity.

Waking up with a glass of tea and a bialy, I dialed the Elizabeth, New Jersey, number. It rang seven times.

"Hello," I shouted.

"You got a phone booth here."

"Where?"

"On Elizabeth Avenue and Broad Street, next to Schulman's dress shop, across from the courthouse."

The familiar Westchester number was busy so I lit a Winston and resolved to take a bus to Elizabeth that afternoon for the one o'clock call. It might be interesting to see who was waiting to answer the phone. It would be a stakeout. I started trying on black T-shirts when the phone rang.

"Soph — where have you been? I've been trying to call you. Dad passed out on the street." It was my brother Lou. "It's not that serious, he'll be back home soon, but the family's still pretty upset. He was just walking to the dentist and fainted in front of the emergency room of University Hospital. They gave him a room on the twelfth floor for

56

tests. Mom really wants you to come over. I think you should. She asked me to call you. I think she'll behave herself, Soph. I can't promise, but I think so."

Sigh. I knew it wasn't going to be easy. But, being my mother's daughter, familial duty weighs heavy on the conscience.

I stumbled into my clothes and down six flights tripping over the three winos who had recently taken up residence on my front stoop. They gurgled as I raced off to the subway.

I dreaded these family emergencies. I dreaded any contact with the family whatsoever, except for Lou of course. He's always been cool. But the parents had reached the point of no return long ago. I'd tried every possible strategy for cease-fire once it became clear that our mutual disapproval wasn't just a phase.

I'd tried fighting: "Just because I don't want to go to Israel does not mean that I am a 'self-hating Jew.' "

I'd tried arguing: "How can you say it's unnatural — can't you see that sexuality is a social construct?"

"Don't social construct me," my mother would say. "Don't give me this social construct," my father would say.

"You're psychopathic," my mother would yell. "You're like a drug addict. All you want is your next shot. You wear your problems like a banner on Fifth Avenue."

When my article *A Jewish Lesbian Speaks* appeared in a progressive magazine, my parents threatened to sell the business and move to New Hampshire. "At least no one will know us there," they said.

Then it came to me one day that I didn't love them. It happened when they hurt me again, and I wasn't surprised. In fact, I expected it. It's made life easier to have a way to measure these things.

Last year I did a late night talk show, midnight to 3 a.m.,

a call-in program. For three hours in between cosmic communicators, a woman who meowed, wrong numbers, inebriated fantasizers and Nazis, an older man with an Eastern European accent kept calling in.

"Kill all gays." Then he would hang up. He must have called twenty times.

A week later I attended the wedding of a Lubuvitche cousin, Rivke, in Crown Heights. Born the same year as me, she was set up in an arranged marriage to a *yeshiva buche* from Israel who she met the day before the wedding. He was a pasty, bitter and pale young man with thick glasses. He was one of those orthodox boys who study from the moment they're able to sit up in a chair. She had to shave her head for the wedding and was wearing the traditional wig of a married woman. The next day the two of them would go off to Israel. At the party following the service, men danced together as befits the passion of the Lubuvitch. The whirling, jumping and kicking went on for hours. Even my father danced on the table. Off in the corner I stood, the perennial observer in drag: my mother's dress and my sister's boots. At least here I could dance with the girls since mixed dancing is forbidden, due, in part, to the natural filthiness of women; but I knew that I still didn't exactly fit in. A large man with a large beard came to speak to me. A surprisingly muscular man for a scholar, he smiled wide and showed his yellow teeth.

"Sophela, I heard you on the radio the other night."

He smiled again.

I looked at him.

He looked at me.

That was the end of my search for my roots.

Now that the autumn weather was turning chilly, the heat had finally been turned off on the subway. Most of the windows were wedged open. Each passenger sat alone, together in the grey boringness. I took a deep breath as the train pulled into the 33rd Street station.

CHAPTER FIFTEEN

I felt a little chill coming on as I waited for the hospital elevator. It's not the Judaism that bothers me, it really is the family. The two are separate in my mind. Judaism and I made our peace last year when I was writing an article on women, orthodoxy and abortion. My photographer, Muffin, another Jewish lez, though a bit more assimilated, decided that we should do some fieldwork. So, one Saturday morning we dutifully prepared to meet with God.

In long sleeves, long skirts and dark stockings, with kerchiefs on our heads, we set off for the Eldridge Street synagogue. Built by Eastern European Jewish immigrants, it had once had a congregation of thousands. Now, its twenty paid members try to keep the roof from falling in on the Italian walls, walnut pews and hand-blown glass gas-lights.

The old *shammes* told us to sit in the back, in the corner. We were the only women. Then they pulled the curtain. Not a light delicate lace curtain between the sexes, but a heavy, dirty, brown canvas curtain that cut us off from the men, the temple, the service and God. As the opening prayer started, we got comfortable. First we took off our hats, then our shoes. Realizing, as women before us must have realized, that the old men, praying to themselves, did not know or care what we were doing, we smiled at each other. I put my hand on Muffin's leg, pulling her skirt up high.

We didn't know each other very well, but I sensed she'd be into it — this private communication with God. It was going to be a game. Muffin and Sophie on their first date. She stared ahead as if nothing was happening, but with a big smile on her face. Just like Andy Feldman in eighth grade, she stretched and yawned, ending up with her hand around my shoulders, inching down under my blouse, closer and closer to my left breast. An interesting moment, two grown-up lesbians sitting in *shul* trying to get to second base. In no time at all she had my shirt unbuttoned like a pro and was trying to unsnap my bra.

"Wait — let me do it," I whispered.

"Listen, I do this a lot, I know how."

Oh no, this would ruin everything. Everybody has something weird about them, some secret shame and mine is my bra. All right, so I wear those old-fashioned ones with under-wire and three rows of hooks. That's how I'm built. My mother didn't consult the fashion mags when she made me. And it doesn't help matters when Lillian calls them "Your World War One underwear." I took it off myself. My breasts felt great in the cool air.

Muffin was agile and dark skinned. The kind of woman my grandmother probably made out with in the potato fields of Lithuania. With a very big smile she came and sat on my lap, facing me. Letting her shirt drop to the floor, she touched by breasts with her own and rubbed her soft, soft cheeks along my face. Her face and breasts felt like one skin. We rocked back and forth as she messily licked my face, starting with wet sloppy ones over my eyes. Then came small kisses, a combination of bites and long romantic ones that make you die a little bit inside. I lowered my face to the space between her breasts, hoping to soak in some more of that fruity waxy smell. I teased her, my specialty, placing my mouth dryly over her nipple, lightly biting it but keeping away my tongue, and then surprising her with the ever so slow long wet strokes and circles. I felt it harden between my lips as Muffin moved with me to the tune of the old men's prayers. As she reached down to stroke the hair between my thighs, my hand was down the back of her skirt. The monotone chanting reverberated through the large and airy synagogue. The light streamed in from the crumbling stained glass windows highlighting the soft hair on Muffin's skin. Everything was cool, light and thrilling, like floating in water. As she pressed her body closer to mine, I felt her relax and I reached into her body, sliding over her asshole, vagina and slithery clitoris with first one finger, then two, then three.

"Shit."

"What's the matter?"

"Sophie, that's the last prayer. I remember from Sunday school in Hewlitt, the service is ending goddammit, hurry up and get your clothes on."

We thanked the *shammes* for letting us have this golden opportunity.

"It was a religious experience," Muffin said.

"I certainly hope so." He smiled, inviting us to come again. Anytime.

Later, I felt really good, I had found my place in Judaism, behind the curtain making love with girls. Not perfect, but no so bad either. As for Muffin, I sent in my story and she sent in her photos. She also sent me a small raincheck, which I've still got in my desk.

CHAPTER SIXTEEN

I entered the hospital room with my mind on other things and forgot to prepare for the hostile faces of my mother and sister. Lou grinned from the corner.

"Hi Dad, how're you doing? I hear you haven't been feeling too well."

He didn't say a word.

"Hi Dad, how's it going?"

Mom took his hand. "Lenny, I know she's a *shanda* but at least you should say hello."

Nothing.

"Lenny, have some grapes. I bought them and washed them. They were one dollar seventy-nine cents, eat them, they're fresh."

My father sat staring, his eyes slightly glassy, with his right forefinger dangling precariously out of the corner of his mouth. It was that Sunday afternoon football game expression.

"So as I was saying," my mother continued. "Cousin Edith is getting married next month to a very nice boy, he's in computers, and Sophie, I want you should know that my beautiful wedding dress which I've saved for you all these years is going to be my wedding gift to her." She emphasized "her." "No use letting such a dress go to waste." Glare.

"But Momma," whined Amy, "What about my wedding?

I could wear your dress at my wedding."

"Amy, don't tell me you're getting married too." I was always the last to know.

"Well, not right away but definitely before I'm twenty-four. I'm sure of that. How old are you now Sophie?"

She annoyed me. Always. Lou and I often wondered out loud how Amy could have lived and functioned for twenty years without ever having expressed an opinion or an idea.

"Yes dear, you'll have a lovely wedding with bridesmaids and fresh flowers."

"How many guests can I invite?" Amy smiled sweetly. I was getting sick.

"As many as you like. You've always been a good girl." Smile. "Not like your sister." Glare.

"Hey Ma, why can't I wear your dress when I get married?" Lou grinned from the corner. That boy knows how to pose.

She ignored his comment as I flashed a thank-you smile.

"Sophie, why don't you get some decent clothes instead of always dressing like a man?"

"Ma, do I really look like a man to you? Look at me." I stuck out my chest.

"Sophie, don't be rude." She turned back to Dad. "Myra's daughter just graduated summa cum laude from Radcliffe. She's going to marry a Harvard boy from a Jewish family in Colorado of all places. They're in oil. Have you ever heard of such a thing as Jews in oil? He's getting his doctorate in advanced particle physics, God knows what that is. Mrs. Long down the hall, her son just finished his degree at Columbia Law School and he graduated twenty-first in his class. Stevie Levy, you remember, his father was your science teacher, Sophie — well, he just finished a Fulbright to Rome where he is studying architectural history. What a lovely boy. I remember he rode his bicycle three

blocks to bring you a valentine's day card. Don't you remember, he was so handsome.''

"Oh," I said.

"Sophia, why can't you be more respectful?"

"Please, Ma, let's not start this now okay? Because I
can't fight with you in a hospital room, so just hold it in
for a few hours then you can call me up and abuse me over
the phone.''

"Don't you tell me what to do. Your problem is that
you never accepted that you're a woman. Your father says
it's all my fault because I took you to see Martin Luther King
and that you hit your head a lot when you were little, the
gay thing I mean. You never think about us, about how
embarrassing it would be if this got back to the family in
Israel. All you ever think about is your own life.''

"Ma —''

"Besides, look at your poor father, he can't do anything
for himself.''

"Ma, he's always like this. Besides, he never does anything for himself, he can't even set the table.''

"Well, he can set part of the table. He knows where the
forks go.''

The conversation was over.

CHAPTER SEVENTEEN

Lou and I sped out towards Elizabeth, New Jersey, in his 1961 Ford Falcon.

"I really appreciate you giving me this lift, brother. I have to get some local color for an article I'm doing on small New Jersey towns and their street corners."

"Sure thing."

Lou's really a good guy for a seventeen-year-old male in 1982 America. He doesn't like to go too deeply into things, mostly because he's so good-hearted, he can't stand to confront realities which are harsh. Most are. He also has an understanding of the war between the sexes which far surpasses that of most mortal men. Unfortunately he knows it, which makes him occasionally intolerable.

"Hey Lou, how's your new girlfriend?" I thought that would be a good typical older sister question.

"She's okay. How's yours?"

"She's okay too."

We drove past the Budweiser Plant toward Elizabeth, another dying American city.

"She's okay Soph except for one thing. She sleeps with her brother."

"Oh."

"I mean, she likes me but she's in love with him."

We sat in silence for a while. I remembered the time I

did a speaking engagement in Staten Island about what it's like to be a lesbian and why people should support the gay rights bill. When I finished speaking and had survived the usual questions like "Do you do it with animals?" One woman stood up and said, "I've never had an orgasm. How do I talk to my children about sex?"

I thought for a moment and then replied in my feminist knight in shining armor voice, "Tell them what you just told me. Tell them the truth about what you know and what you don't know. Speak from the reality of your experience. It'll be the most helpful information you can share with your children." The audience had exploded into wild applause.

"Lou, I just don't know what to say."

"I didn't think you would."

We were late. It drove me crazy. I can't stand to be one second late, not for a movie, a class, to meet a friend, nothing. I ruins my whole week. "Can't you drive any faster?"

"No Soph, are you going to pay the speeding ticket?"

I sat back in my seat and chewed on a Virginia Slim.

We turned off the highway onto Elizabeth Avenue. A hundred years ago, this town was one of the poor northern centers of the Ku Klux Klan. Later, Jews, escaping from the Lower Eastside, came here to start small businesses. Now Blacks and Hispanic people inhabit this spot in the heart of the leukemia belt, downwind from the asbestos factories of Northern New Jersey. We drove past a dilapidated movie theatre playing *Five Fingers of Death* and *The Gore-Gore Girls,* up to the corner phone booth.

The courthouse clock said 1:05. Shit. We waited a few more minutes, but knowing what I already knew about the kind of company Seymour kept, they were never late. In those five minutes whoever it was probably came and went. That is if they hadn't heard the news about Seymour's murder. That is if they hadn't *made* the news about Seymour's murder.

Dejected, I suggested to Lou that we find some food. We drove around for a while until it became clear that if there had ever been a deli in town, it wasn't there now. We pulled into a Pizza Hut and ordered. Sitting over mushroom pizza and Sprite, we shot the shit. I bummed a Kool from the cashier.

"Hey Soph, let's go play video games."

"I don't want to."

"You know Sophie, I've noticed something about you. You don't like change. You want to eat the same food and read the same books and play the same games you've always played. You never want to do anything modern like disco roller-skating or play video games."

"That's not true. I'm very up-to-date, I'm hip, I'm with what's happening, I have to be in my business. What kind of reporter do you think I would be if I didn't keep up to the most recent minute?"

We chose Ms. Pac-Man, a bone for each of us. First you put a quarter in and then the computer sings a little mechanized theme song. Suddenly Ms. Pac-Man appears on the electronic screen. She's in a maze. She has to gobble up as many little blue dots as she can before the monsters catch her. It's social-realism about women and over-eating. In about thirty seconds, the monsters had caught me three times and my turn was over.

"That's all you get for a quarter? What a rip-off."

"No Soph, you didn't do it right — watch."

Like a pro, my little brother smoothly manipulated Ms. Pac-Man in and out, dodging, weaving. It took all his concentration but she ate all the little blue dots.

"What happens now?"

"Watch."

It was intermission. We heard the theme song again and then the Ms. Pac-Man and a new figure appeared.

"Who's that?"

"That's Mister Pac-Man. They're going to get married."

Sure enough, the two little Pac-People merged and reproduced miniature Pac-ettes.

"I can't stand it, compulsory heterosexuality, it's all over the place."

I sat down and waited for Lou to finish. "Lou, you've got mozzarella on your ear."

"Kids really like these games Soph. Some kids in my school are addicted to it. They play video games twelve hours a day. They cut school and steal money just so they can play video games."

"What ever happened to basketball? Lou, if you don't start doing those normal teenage things you're going to be bald and fat before your time."

"Bald, do you think I'm balding?"

"No, silly, don't worry, it was just an idle threat."

"Besides Soph, I've got more important things to think about."

"Like what?"

"Like herpes."

I ordered another Sprite. Lou ordered another pizza. He's a growing boy.

In the ladies room I washed my hands and face and tried to get the tomato sauce off my shirt. I mulled over the evolution of this peculiar story. Things weren't exactly going great. I stared at myself in the mirror. Here I am, a twenty-four-year-old dyke. I took inventory: brown hair, brown eyes, full Jewish lips, just like Ethel Rosenberg. Most of my girlhood friends are married or in professional school, or at least working nine to five and certainly not talking to me about it.

Times are hard. They always have been hard for most

people and in my line of life they always will be for me too. Will I ever be able to earn a decent living, have nice clothes, keep my hair combed? Will I spend the rest of my life running around after women I'm not going to get and stories that no one's going to appreciate?

"I love your articles," one woman told me at a party, "but they're so long I never get past the fourth paragraph. Five paragraphs is enough to explain anything. Don't you think so?"

"Oh," I said.

I became increasingly aware of someone looking at me in the mirror. I caught her reflection in the eye.

"Hello Sophie."

Those brutal grey flashing eyes, those proletarian shoes, that Palestinian scarf. There was no doubt about it.

"Germaine." I could barely get it out.

"You think you're a piece of hot shit, don't you Sophie?"

"Germaine what are you doing here at Pizza Hut? Did you escape from the FBI? I thought you were a prisoner of the state."

"Shows what kind of detective you are. We followed you here from the phone booth. You drove around a while trying to shake us, didn't you? Don't try to shake me Sophie."

"I was just looking for a corned beef on rye. What do you mean *we* followed you? Who is we?"

"We watched you slink around in that stained black T-shirt like Sam Spade, making a fool out of yourself."

Times hadn't changed Germaine Covington. "Listen to me Sophie. You're messing around in something bigger than you are. We know you killed Seymour Epstein and if you don't stay out of our business, we're not going to be the only ones who know it."

"Wait a minute . . ."

She waited. I didn't know what to say, the girl's timing was impeccable, and I was in serious trouble. Any jerk could've figured that out. I tried to be smart. "Wait a minute Germaine. How do I know it wasn't you? I know it wasn't me. How do you have all this information anyway?" I couldn't decide if I should try to play it cool or fall on my knees and beg for mercy. Something about her made you want to do that.

"Wait Germaine. I shouldn't ask that of you. I mean, you're a woman who's been underground for twelve years. While I was buying my first training bra, you were traveling in China and Cuba and North Viet Nam — you've survived, you're strong."

She really was magnificent, even if she was a bitch. Neither could be denied. And those grey eyes really did flash, just like Seymour said in his *Voice* article. He must have talked to her after all.

"Oh don't be so naive Sophie, it's not as great as you think. Don't you read *Rolling Stone*? Years of being afraid, false identification, not being able to make new friends, in a sense making a commitment not to grow as a person, only as a political entity. Waiting, hoping, giving everything to build a movement and watching that movement crumble leaving people's lives as hard as they were before. Betraying all their faith in the possibility of change. Paying our bills on time, being afraid to cross a red light. Does that sound romantic to you?"

"No, I guess not."

I took another look. Her eyes were tired. Her hair had streaks of grey, but not too many.

"Germaine, please tell me what's going on. Did you escape from the FBI? Were you at that bank at all?"

"Think a minute Sophie. That doesn't really matter anymore, does it?"

"I don't get it."

"Even if you think otherwise, all the rest of America knows that Germaine Covington is dead. She died in jail of a drug overdose, self-administered, of course."

"So?"

"So, now I'm free, it's over. I can go where I want and live the way I want. Germaine is dead and I need your help to keep it that way. Sophie, forget about this story. Let me die in peace."

I looked at her, feeling something between us, wondering if she felt anything at all. That Germaine — she sure knew how to make you want to give her her way. It was almost a skill.

"You have my word Germaine. I won't betray you. Your story is safe with me." I felt like riding off into the sunset.

She dried her hands on a paper towel and stepped into a vacant stall.

"But, Germaine, just tell me one thing." I spoke through the closed door. "Who did kill Seymour Epstein? Just for my own curiosity of course. What happened at the bank, and by the way, where is Laura Wolfe?"

There was no answer. I looked under the door. No feet. I crawled in. The window was open. She was gone.

CHAPTER EIGHTEEN

I got home that afternoon looking as if I'd seen my own ghost in the mirror. The three winos were still sitting on my stoop. While I fumbled for my keys, one of them lifted his head.

"Miss Horowitz?"

"Yes?"

"We're from the FBI." He wasn't gurgling.

That's how I ended up alone in my sixth floor walk-up with three FBI agents dressed as smelly winos. Well, I wasn't exactly alone. Evan was there of course, but he just sat in the corner pulling hairs out of the middle of his head. The agents paced back and forth in my living room. It's about ten by twelve, so, with their New England prep school strides, they could easily take about two steps in any direction.

"Miss Horowitz. We have information, a signed affidavit from Frances Mary Marino that you have been fraternizing with known opponents of the democratic system."

So the animals had found my waitress.

"We know you are withholding information vital to the security and safety of your fellow Americans."

I tried to imagine him having sex with a twelve-year-old boy.

"Now Miss Horowitz. You can cooperate like a good citizen and tell us what you know."

A good citizen. It had a vaguely familiar ring. In girl scouts I'd earned a good citizen badge by serving as color guard, reciting the pledge of allegiance and learning how to properly fold and burn a flag that had touched ground. The latter skill did come in handy. We had to memorize the four freedoms. Freedom of speech, freedom of religion, freedom of the press . . .

"I'm a reporter and my notes are protected under freedom of the press."

"Miss Horowitz, I'm sorry to disappoint you but we are not playing any games here. So why don't you just keep that liberal crap to yourself."

"I am not a liberal."

"A bank was robbed. One of the women involved in this incident is currently a fugitive. We have reason to believe that you have information concerning her whereabouts."

"I think I need to call my lawyer."

They sat down and waited. Three FBI men squeezed together on my second-hand futon. Over their heads hung an *In Celebration of Amazons* poster announcing the Midwest Lesbian Arts and Music Festival.

I knew two lawyers. One was Barbara Hubbard, the nationally renowned feminist lawyer. She was beautiful, a dedicated woman with a head of grey, blue, black thick hair that looked like a stormy ocean. As the battles grew longer and harder, she started getting wearier. She would sit in meetings, trancelike with a dull, practiced smile on her face. A strong woman, whose commitment to losing causes had made her inaccessible as a human being. It made her exist, apart from and in a sense, above, all petty human conflict. The only other lawyer I knew was Eva. In 11th grade when we were making out in the girls' bathroom, she promised me I could always count on her. "Winter, Spring, Summer or Fall, all you gotta do is call" she wrote in my high school yearbook.

In the background I heard Evan talking to the agents. "WOW, are you guys really in the FBI? How do you get into it? Do you have to take a test? I'm pretty smart, you know, I used to be a child prodigy." I resolved to get rid of him as soon as possible.

The phone rang twice, it was after six, she should be home making dinner for her little hubby.

"Eva, it's Sophie. Please don't hang up. There are three FBI men sitting here on my futon and I need a lawyer and you're the only one I know. I don't want you to think I've done anything wrong . . ."

"I know all about it. I'm working for the Westchester D.A. now, for Peter Pope. They're going to serve you with a Grand Jury subpoena as soon as you hang up this phone. I advise you to tell them everything. If you have nothing to hide then don't hide anything. Don't call me any more. Sophie, grow up."

I stood making rhythmic yes sounds into the dial tone. It had a calming effect, the drone that follows the click that terminates an unpleasant conversation. I pondered the mysteries of life: My old girlfriend is a fink for the cops. I'm about to go to jail for information I don't have. Peter Pope, the name on Seymour's bank statements is the Westchester D.A. Isn't life so full of surprises, it makes you want to vomit?

"My lawyer says I don't have to answer your questions." They handed me the subpoena and left.

CHAPTER NINETEEN

Sometimes life makes you laugh. Sometimes life makes you cry. Sometimes life makes you sick to your stomach. This was one of those times.

I went to the bathroom. Evan had of course left piss on the floor and all over the toilet seat. Weren't fathers supposed to teach their sons these things? "Here little Evan-Wevan, first you lift up the seat and then you hold your little weanie so your pee-pee doesn't invade everybody else's life."

Evan blew his nose and left the tissues on the floor.

I walked into the living room. I sat on the chair. I screamed at the top of my lungs, "I'm sick and tired of you, you stupid, disgusting asshole, jerk fuckface, idiot. You yuchy FBI lover, piss all over the floor, ketchup sucking mongrel, you smell bad, and you're ugly and you stink. Get out of my house and never come back — do you hear me!"

Evan didn't know what to do. He held his head still, pointed in my direction, opened his mouth in a gape of horror and moved his eyes back and forth looking for some way out. Then he collapsed back in his chair and started to cry. Snot was dripping from his nose as his shrieks became more and more sorrowful. He wiped it off on the curtains. I took a drag off a Salem Light. I was considering switching to menthol.

Okay, so I was scared. It's not so terrible to be petrified with fear. It's good for me to feel things that deeply. Why shouldn't I be scared to death? I had to get a grip on things. I needed to find a lawyer. I had to calm down. What would make me calm? Maybe I should think about what I was going to do that week. On Thursday I'd see Vivian. That should be nice. I had sort of a soft spot for her. But that was Thursday, this was Tuesday. What could I do that would take my mind off all this trouble? I could read a book. I looked at my books. *Inside the Third Reich*, that was a good book. I could take another look at Seymour's papers.

The bank statements were at the top of the pile. They were from the White Plains Bank detailing a series of small but regular deposits. None exceeded five hundred dollars. Those pennies do add up eventually though. The balance seemed to hover around seventy-five thou. Enough to keep Seymour in leather, coke, boys and more. I couldn't keep my mind on the evidence. That blasted typing from across the way was getting on my nerves. I moved into the living room and started perusing the clippings on my walls. Yep, there it was in the newspaper of record:

> Peter Pope, Westchester District Attorney, personally presided over the arraignment of Miss Covington.

I bet he did. These might have been the documents stolen from the bank. Pretty slick. I poured myself a Spatan Dark and went over the sequence of events. But that typing, it was really bothering me. Making me nervous. So much was happening. I needed space to think.

Evan had finished crying and was now cooking some foul concoction in the kitchen. His ugly face was all red. The smell was creeping into my brain. The typing from across the alley pounding away, the Bob Dylan music in the background, Evan in my kitchen, I just couldn't take it one minute longer. I ran to the window.

"Will you stop that fucking typing!"

It stopped. I lit a cigarette. The phone rang.

"Miss Horowitz?" It was a sweet old voice.

"Yes?"

"Hello Miss Horowitz. I'm afraid that I'm the typing culprit. I think perhaps, if you're not too busy, you might pop over and we could discuss this matter further, drink some tea and have a little chat."

"Look, I'm sorry that I yelled at you, I'm sure you're very nice, but I've had a bad day and it's hard for me to concentrate."

"I know you've had a difficult afternoon," she replied sympathetically. "What a shame to have those three policemen waiting outside your building. You must be terribly distraught.

"How did you know they were policemen? How did you know they weren't winos?"

"My dear, I couldn't help but notice their ruddy complexions. Like a ski weekend in Vail. They had good figures, not at all under-nourished like those poor fellows we've been seeing so much more of lately. Furthermore, Miss Horowitz ..."

"Yes?"

"They always seem to be intoxicated, but they never drank anything besides coffee. Just sat there and gurgled like babies."

"I'll be right over Mrs. . . . ."

"Noseworthy."

"I'll be right over."

CHAPTER TWENTY

"Do come in Miss Horowitz. I've been interested in meeting you."

"Oh, do you read *Feminist News*?"

"No, no, heavens no."

She was, what else can I say, a little old lady. Not too old, but old nevertheless. Her hair was grey, her face was wrinkled, her dress went down below her knee. Her house was covered with books. Thousands of books. On the shelves, on the tables and chairs and floor. And none of these books looked familiar. They were all paperbacks — the kind that women read on the subway, with strange names like *Murder in the Men's Room.* Then there were more books, the kind that mechanics carry around in their back pockets or physics students read under the covers with titles like *Bulika, Chief of the Trayules.*

"Have we met before?"

"No dear. I've just observed some very nice people coming and going from your apartment. You seem to have some good kind friends who always look happy. All except for that poor wretched little bastard who's sleeping in your kitchen."

I looked out her window directly into my apartment. She was one flight higher, so I couldn't look back.

"Would you care for some tea?"

"Would you happen to have anything stronger? I've had a hard day."

"Old Grand Dad?"

It hit the spot. She was a nice lady after all, even if she was a bit snoopy. Probably had nothing better to do all day than read these trash novels. I noticed that one whole case was filled with books by King James, that writer Lillian liked so much.

"You like King James, don't you?"

"I am King James."

She smiled and I caught the twinkle of pleasure in her eye. "Sophie, I know you must be a little surprised, but don't underestimate me because I have grey hair. We needn't be macho to be powerful my dear. I've been writing science fiction, detective novels and fantasy pieces for over forty years. Seven hours a day, six days a week. Now I'm working on my five hundred and twenty-fifth novel. It should be quite a good one too. Now, Sophie, I know you have gotten into some kind of trouble and let me say for the record that although I don't enjoy politics very often, I do find the government rather unpleasant and the individuals that comprise it rather the same. So, I assume that if one of those horrid men is bothering you, you might be doing, as they say, something right."

So I told her the story. I needed someone to talk to about it anyway and she seemed to be the one. I told her the whole story from the radio announcement at the Key Food to Germaine's appearance at the Pizza Hut and all the sordid details in between. She sat quietly the whole time, rocking in her rocking chair and stroking the neck of her cat. I finished with Seymour's papers and sat back exhausted, taking the liberty of pouring some more Old Grand Dad.

"So, what do you think?"

She took off her spectacles and laid them on the coffee

table. "Sophie, I think you are a good and courageous young woman, but you are, unfortunately, an amateur. You have overlooked some very important evidence."

"Not inconceivable."

"Well, if this Seymour chap and this Germaine character, her poor, unfortunate stand-in and the District Attorney, Mister Pope, are all in, shall we say, cahoots, we need to examine why. Why would Mister Pope work with such an unseemly figure as Mister Epstein? The answer lies, I believe, in the cache of stolen goods found in the apartment after the murder. If Seymour was what is commonly known as a fence, he had to get those goods from somewhere. Germaine wouldn't be the person for that, too risky for a woman in her position — but who better than a district attorney for access to stolen merchandise? Do you see?"

I saw.

"I assume Mr. Pope felt that his moment of reckoning was approaching, an investigation or the like, and he desperately needed to destroy any records of bank deposits that might connect him to Mister Epstein. So, they developed a bank robbery, the investigation of which would conveniently be supervised by —"

"By the D.A. of course. This would be a great story. How do I pin it on him, Mrs. Noseworthy? Can you help me?"

"Ah — Sophie, this is one of those times when the *sagesse* of old age becomes a valuable item. You need to ask yourself some questions Sophia. You need to ask yourself why."

"Why?"

"Why do you want to expose Mister Pope? What will it bring to your own life? What insights will it give you? Do you really want to be the kind of writer who exposes politicians and covers boring crime and corruption?"

I looked at the floor.

"I thought not. Or would you rather transcend the interchangeable facts of daily existence and everyday events to capture and address the higher moral questions of human commitment, desire and ability? Do you see Sophia, your interest is in Laura Wolfe, because something in her story touches your own experience. This I can understand immediately. Looking for Laura Wolfe is a personal journey for you and I advise you to continue it. I would, however, be careful of that gentleman, the Asian physician who appears to be so helpful. No District Attorney has the power to force a doctor to inject a patient with Thorazine against the doctor's medical judgment, at least not in a public hospital. It's just not done. I'm afraid Dr. Tsang has offered you some misleading information."

"Well, Mrs. Noseworthy, your ideas about Seymour and the D.A. are good ones, but I know Henry well. Maybe he's covering up some feelings that he didn't act responsibly, but I don't think he would consciously mislead me."

"Sophie, no one ever has the right answer to every situation. Even Henrietta Bell, my greatest detective, makes mistakes. Here's a copy of one of her adventures. I hope you enjoy it. I do wish you the best and urge you to be prudent in your judgments. As for me, I'm afraid I need now to return to my typewriter. I hope your new state of mind will make the typing more tolerable. I've only just moved here temporarily from my home in Nantucket. It's only for a few months while the renovations are done. My son lives here normally. He's a musician. He plays with a group of fine spirited young people who call themselves Beverly Hell and the Five Towns. Have you ever heard of them? They're quite clever."

"Well, yes Mrs. Noseworthy, I saw them just a few weeks ago. They're very good."

"He's staying at his boyfriend's house until I can go home to New England. So, Sophie, we both must return to our work. I hope we can take tea again before I return to Cape Cod." She showed me to the door.

"Yes, yes you've really been great. Thanks for everything. Bye."

It had been a long day. I crawled into bed with a copy of *Murder in the Missionary Position* and fell fast asleep.

CHAPTER TWENTY-ONE

We walked through the zoo and into the park. The trees were full and overgrown deep green everywhere. The cold air and thick brush hid the litter and created a pastoral scene as Vivian Beck and I strolled past the skating rink. Spray-painted on a tunnel in faded red letters was PNOM PENH'S GONNA FALL.

"Some archaeologist should rescue that relic." Vivian laughed.

"I have some vague memory of those anti-war marches," I interjected, trying to meet Vivian on her own turf. "My mother used to take us. I didn't really understand the chants, so I'd make up my own. Like 'Ho-Ho-Ho-Chi-Minh, the NFL is Gonna Win,' I never knew if that was for the North Vietnamese or the New York Giants."

Vivian was wearing fall colors. Soft browns and reds and olive green carefully arranged for effect. It had an effect.

"How old are you Sophie?"

"Twenty-four. How old are you?"

"Thirty-four."

"That means you were twenty-four in -uh —"

"Nineteen seventy-three."

She looked quiet. I didn't want to lose the moment. "So, we've both been young in difficult times. It must have been a disappointment for you after all that excitement and hope. It must have been hard to figure out where you were going next."

"Oh Sophie, you're so cute. I'm afraid you're romanticizing a bit though. You know, for some of my friends, nothing interesting has happened since nineteen seventy-two. It's all they've got to hold on to to prove that sometime in their lives they were vibrant. It's taken almost a decade for me to realize that nothing is going to turn the world over for me and I'm wasting my time if I sit around waiting. I have to make my own decisions now, I'm not going to be saved by social unrest, I don't know if you understand what I'm saying. Is your life exciting for you?"

"Well, when I'm on a story and have something neat to do it's great. I love running around sleazy parts of town, developing contacts and information sources, hanging out with all kinds of people, but it's usually for a story. Sometimes I think I'd stay home all day and cry if I wasn't working on a project."

I was worried she would think I was a punk in my sneakers and blue jeans. I'm not a kid anymore. Does she see me as a woman or a cute little boy or an androgyne or a friend? Vivian's eyes were as green as her sweater. Her lips looked soft. We were sitting in a small boat house by the rowboat lake. Behind us was The Ramble. A lone boat quietly passed by.

"It's like sitting on the Connecticut River," Vivian said. "I haven't done that since I was a girl." She looked out over the water. She turned to face me.

I wanted to kiss her. We looked at each other. I wanted to kiss her soft so she would know what that's like and then kiss her hard so she wouldn't think that soft was the only option.

"Sophie, what do you think about this murder that everyone's talking about — Seymour Epstein?"

I didn't know what to say.

"I mean, I knew him from the old days, though we haven't talked in years, except over the deli counter at Zabar's. But I was so shocked at his death. You're a reporter. I thought you might have heard something."

"They think it's some kind of gay-pick-up-combination-murder. At least that's what the dailies are saying. Why, what do you think Vivian?"

I was thinking that I was a real jerk. Here I had deceived myself into believing that she liked me but really she only wanted to find out about Seymour.

"It could have been anyone. Seymour wasn't well liked in any circle. You can be terminally obnoxious for only so long without getting someone really angry."

"So, Vivian, you think it was a personal revenge thing?"

"Well, Sophie, don't quote me now, but it has occurred to me that . . . well, of course, I don't know anything more than what I've told you, but neither do you. It's getting chilly, I should be heading back to Westchester, it's so strange living in suburbia when I'm so used to the Upper Westside. You know, I totally forgot to bring you those pictures of Laura. They're still sitting on my kitchen table. We really should get together again some day and go over them. You know, I really enjoy these talks we've had. It's made me think about things I've successfully avoided confronting for ten years. I wish I could find Laura and talk to her about it. You haven't heard from her have you? All right then."

She gave me a peck on the cheek and disappeared into the mist dividing the tall grey buildings from the park.

I sat by the lake for a moment. There was no doubt about it, I had a serious crush on Vivian Beck. She just seemed so ripe for it. I couldn't restrain myself. It's such a special thrill, getting involved with straight women. My friends think I'm crazy because it's so dangerous, between their freak-outs and angry boyfriends, but I know that they're also grateful and that's very delicious. Even if they run screaming into the arms of their old man waiting in the car, you've become someone they can never forget. Besides, nothing beats the pure pleasure of watching them experience women in such an immense way for the first time. It's a thrill, almost a fetish. Some people are into little boys, others like leather. I happen to prefer straight women, it's my sexuality and Vivian was going to be tough, but not impossible.

Now, it's not every straight woman in the world. Just the ones who seem never to have made heterosexuality their home, who want something more in their lives but can't imagine what. It's also the thing of taking something away from men, beating them out when they have everything on their side. Vivian's probably been thinking about Laura and what went wrong in their relationship. She's probably evaluating a lot of things. But I knew she liked me, I could just tell. She wouldn't have suggested getting together again if she didn't. Besides, she said that she liked being with me. I just had to play my cards right. I pulled up the collar on my black cloth jacket and started the long walk home.

CHAPTER TWENTY-TWO

"Sophie, you are out of your mind. It's the sad, sad truth. Why, why, why do you insist, against my advice, on wasting your time fooling around at all hours of the day and night with straight women, who have no intention of changing their ways? Hmmm?"

"Chris, I can't help it. I'm into it, I'm a fool for love."

Chris and I were having dinner at her place after a long collective meeting at *Feminist News*.

"Don't bullshit me gorgeous, we've been friends for a long time and I can remember a whole slew of hets of every size and color that you've chased around New York. How about that one who got married?"

"Well, that was an exception."

"How about the one who took you to California and abandoned you on Valencia Boulevard for a guy with a Porsche headed towards L.A.? What was that one, Sophie? By the way, who did you call collect from San Francisco in the middle of the night asking to be wired two hundred dollars with which to crawl home? Hmmmm?"

"Chris, I know you're Black but you remind me of my mother sometimes."

"It's a *shmatta*."

"You mean a *shandra*."

"Oh yeah, I forgot. Anyway Sophie Horowitz, I want

to make it clear now and forever that if you get fucked over by one more straight woman I am not helping you out. *Entiendes?*"

"Yeah, yeah."

"Don't look so hurt Sophie, I know you love me because I tell you what to do. Anyway, Lillian's a very special girl. She's sweet, you should hang on to her, she's a good woman and this Vivian sounds like trouble."

"You know Chris, sometimes you're so old-fashioned. If I get involved with Vivian it won't have any effect on Lillian and me. One has nothing to do with the other. Anyway, don't forget about Laura Wolfe, she's part of this too."

"That reminds me to tell you to keep away from that Laura Wolfe as well. Girl, don't you remember when she and her gang busted up the *Feminist News* community meeting last year chanting *struggle, struggle, struggle?* What's wrong with you Sophie? All you want is trouble. You're never happy with what you got."

"It's too boring."

"There you go sweetheart with your endearing convenient contradictions. After a full day of your one-thrill-after-another life you won't even taste my carefully prepared Haitian spices."

"I only like salt."

"Oh Goddess."

Chris had picked that up from the In Celebration of the Womb Moon conference that she covered in the spring. I started fumbling for a cigarette.

"Here Sophie, have a banana instead. You know I don't want you to die."

"Oh Chrissy, just one, be nice, you know I have to be in court tomorrow."

"You're right. Are you nervous?"

"Well, the clerk told me not to worry right away. This is just an appearance to set a court date. I don't know exactly what to expect though. I've never been in court before except as press."

"Well I'll tell you," Chris answered, digging into her dinner, "I have a story like that, it's not very anything, but I'll tell you anyway. It's not big Black revolutionary and it's not tough Black street kid."

"Chris, cut the crap, I know you're the average woman on the street. What are you eating anyway?"

"Chebri — goat, it's delicious."

"Well, perhaps slightly eccentric."

"Well Sophie, we all seem to have our ethnocentricities, don't we?"

She took another bite and sat back in her familiar I've-got-a-story-position, fork suspended in midair, left hand wildly gesticulating, leaning farther and farther over the table, dramatically pausing for a drink of water. "I was in college. A snotty college. A white college. The board had decided to give a bullshit award to some famous person in order to boost the endowment, so they chose Robert McNamara, you know, the architect of the Viet Nam war. They gave him an award for a 'lifetime contribution to international understanding.' It was too much for even the complacent students of the late seventies. 'Seventy-seven I think it was. So we formed a student protest committee to plan a demonstration. Most of the kids had never done anything remotely like that before and those who had were a little rusty. Being the only Black gay woman, I, of course, got immediately drafted onto every committee and speakers list. You know, 'We've got Chris so no more girls, negroes or faggots.' Of course all the white boys gave big boring speeches about nothing and all this time, while they were talking, McNamara was getting his award across the street. So, when it was my turn, and honey, you know I was last, I said I thought we should stop the yakking and go tell Mister M. what we think about him. Let him sweat a little too. So we did, all one thousand of us. The police came of course and filled up one paddy wagon. I was in it. They charged us with mob action, disorderly conduct and resisting arrest. We ended up in Cook County jail — this is Chicago — which, take my word for it, ain't Old McDonald's Farm. So we walk into the women's section. Eight white women and me and everyone in that prison was black. They hooted and shouted "What are you doing here? You don't belong here,' and when they saw me, bringing up the rear, they didn't know what to say. Well, that made me mad because I may have made the mistake of going to a snotty white college, but I am a proud Black woman and I was determined to find out what was happening. I talked to those women all that night and all the next day until the provost of the college came to get us out. None of them were criminals you know, they were mostly in there for prostitution or passing bad checks or something minor. Well, weeks later when we came to court, the room was filled with about eighty people, each waiting for their one and a half minutes of American justice. I saw one woman I recognized and went over to talk with her. Well, we hadn't even said our hellos when her fat white pimp comes over and starts hollering 'I don't want you fraternizin' with no colored trash' and she was a Black woman. So, anyway, later I went to visit her once. She lived in a housing project on the west side of Chicago called Cabrini Green. It was built as a series of high rises and each apartment had a balcony overlooking the slums of Chicago. But, the crime rate was so high there that the city came and covered the buildings with wire mesh so no one could get in from the outside. Well, you know what? The place looked like a collection of giant hamster cages with poor black people inside running on that wheel. So that's what it was like. Don't you worry Sophie, you know I love you, but they'll never put you in jail for more than overnight. You just don't have the right characteristics."

CHAPTER TWENTY-THREE

Chris finished eating and we started walking over to the Unitarian Church where some women were performing a "Night of Black Lesbian Voices."

"So what else is happening in your life Chrissie? You seem a little troubled."

"Well, do you really want to know?"

"Sure."

"Well, I'm seeing this boy, I don't know, he's very sweet with a feminine face, he hardly looks like a man at all, just like a little boy. I really don't know how this happened, we just started talking at a party and I thought, shit, I spend so much time in these important, transforming relationships, why can't I just do something that's fun? He's very feminist, he's real feminist, reads all the books. He's always saying things to me about how women are naturally superior, he's very sweet. But, unfortunately, he's boring. What do you think?"

"Chris, you're not going straight on me are you? I don't want to hear on the grapevine that you've started a group called Former Lesbians, or that you're married and moved to the suburbs."

"No, no I'm a confirmed woman-loving, cunt-sucking lesbian, I'm just playing around."

"All right then, I hope you have a good time. How many times have you slept with him?"

"Once."

"So what are you worrying about?"

"Oh Sophie, you know how some women are, and I don't blame them really. They've fought so hard to be able to be out of the closet. It's scary to think that someone is buckling under the pressure, but this trick isn't about pressure." Her hands were shoved deep in her pockets as we walked along.

"Chrissie, I didn't say anything about that, why have you been getting a lot of shit lately?"

"I don't know. I know I felt a need that led me to this guy, I had decided to sleep with a man and I was attracted to him first, but there was more to that need than sexual desire."

"Well, don't worry yourself to death over it. You know, Chrissie, even I have fantasies about men sometimes."

"Even super-dyke? You're shitting me."

"That's the truth. Beautiful, vague fantasies about men who make love like women. But I know that even though I can think about it, if I ever got there again with a real man, I don't think I would really want to be there. I'm used to that skin you love to touch, I couldn't transfer to beards and bones."

The front steps were packed with women waiting to get into the church. When I went to white events I knew mostly everyone there. But after a few years of coming to Black women's things I still felt like a fly on the wall. All around me were women whose names and faces were familiar from book jacket covers. Sometimes I just felt pale and plain. Why would anyone here want to talk to a shmuck like me? It was easier to just sit quiet and not make any mistakes.

Walking home all high and excited, we headed towards Vesselka's Polish Home Cooking for some boiled beef with horseradish sauce and a chocolate egg cream.

"Chrissie, it's so weird to be here. This is where Laura Wolfe used to hang out. I'd come in here to read the paper and have coffee in the morning and she'd be sitting over in that corner arguing, or struggling with whomever. All the time, we used to glare at each other. Now she's gone and East Village life continues as if she'd never been here, as if she'd been just plucked out of the scenery."

"Don't get too nostalgic too quickly Sophie, there are some of those Women Against Bad Things at the table behind you."

I turned around. They saw me, collectively. What could they possibly have against me now? I'd written that little piece on Laura for the paper and everyone knew I was working on a bigger one. I was certainly more sympathetic towards their fallen comrade than anybody else was. Those girls, they'd probably forgotten how to smile and thought that's what they were doing.

As a unit, they rose from their table and walked over to where we were sitting. One came forward and looked me in the eye.

"Sisters, we must struggle to move forward. Take our leaflet." She handed me five sheets of legal paper stapled together. Both sides of each sheet were crammed with single spaced typing.

"Don't tell me, it's the new mobilization against egg creams."

"Sisters, this communique explains that we disassociate ourselves from Laura Wolfe because she is an individualist, opportunist, adventurist and doesn't understand the meaning of struggle."

"You're not supporting Laura Wolfe? I'm shocked. No I'm not. She's the best thing that ever happened to you little twerps."

I was surprised at how mad I was getting, but it was true. Even if Laura Wolfe is sort of a jerk, she's had a hard time.

No one has ever had the courage to really love her. Besides, she's courageous, she did what she needed to do even though she didn't get any support for it. She's a good woman. Yes, I felt comfortable saying that. Laura Wolfe is my sister . . . so to speak.

"That's a pretty shitty way to treat your friends," Chrissy responded.

"It's not a question of friends. It's a political question. It's a question of comrades. Who are you anyway? I think you must be an agent."

"That's right, you little bitch, I'm an agent of the devil."

It had been a hard day all around. "Chris, I have to go home. I have to go to court tomorrow. I can't believe how many places I'm in in one day. I feel like five different people."

"Well, it's that New York state of mind."

"Yeah."

"Look Sophie, you don't have to get everything together at once. Just get through tomorrow, I'm sure you'll get a postponement. I'll be sending you love vibes."

"Thanks honey, good night."

"Goodnight."

CHAPTER TWENTY-FOUR

I spent Friday morning at the library reviewing old newspapers. Yep, Mrs. Noseworthy was right. Peter Pope had recently been under investigation concerning the disappearance of stolen property. It all made sense to me. Pope passed the goods on to Seymour who sold them through the black market and kicked back some profit to the D.A. via the White Plains bank. When the investigation got too hot, they set up this robbery to get the records and destroy them.

No wonder Laura Wolfe was hiding out. Poor kid, she probably knew too much for her own good. But how did she get into this mess in the first place? I was starting to grow fond of her. I remembered all the times she screamed at me and told me I was unprincipled. She'd send me three flyers every time her group had a meeting, and call me too. Once I did go. It lasted four hours. When I tried to leave after three, there were four of her girls at the door telling me I was unprincipled. The next day I saw her in the street.

"Hi Laura, how was the end of the meeting?"

"That's not the real question. The real question is why you weren't there."

Chris' way of dealing with them was that every time one of "those girls" would come up to her she'd ask, "Hey Laura, want to lend me five dollars?"

Still, it didn't seem so bad in retrospect. I guess I have been unprincipled in my time, and I did have to admire the way she hung in there when all her friends finked out. I remembered her slogan *Ho-Ho-Ho-Mo-Sexual, The Ruling Class Is Ineffectual.* I repeated it to myself as I entered the lawyer's office on 41st and Madison.

My lawyer's name was June Honeymoon, I found her through Lawyers for the Left. Like many of her comrades she was a divorce lawyer with a prosperous private practice on Central Park West. Her husband paraded himself as a liberal judge. Every three or four years she did a big splashy political case for free (*pro bono* she liked to say) thereby renewing her radical credentials. This was 1982 though and not many big splashy political cases were coming along so she'd agreed to take mine. Something about her manner told me we weren't going to get along. I think I started off with a bad attitude when I saw her office. It was arranged to be stylishly simple with plexiglass furniture, area lighting and no books.

"Susan," she said, "I've reviewed your files and I think we can win this. Just trust me and you won't have to spend a minute in jail. What we need now is a theory of defense."

She frowned a moment, as if deep in thought. "I've got it. We'll argue that you didn't know it was illegal."

"Wait a minute."

"Now Susan, I know you believe in consensus and all that, but things are breaking fast, sometimes we just have to go with the current. Just believe me, I know what's best. My senior partner John Snort will argue the case. He carries a lot of weight with the judges."

"Sophie. My name is Sophie and I want one thing to be clear from the beginning. I don't want a man arguing my case in court. Men are welcome to help out and I would be grateful if they do but I feel it's important for a feminist to be defended by a woman. That's why I chose your name out of the directory. I want a woman counsel." I liked the sound of that word counsel, like I knew what I was talking about.

"Look Susan, you are not considering the different factors in this very complex case. I am not implying that I am not qualified to represent you because I most certainly am. However, I also am capable of putting the best interests of my client before any petty personal desire for success as an attorney. My job is to get you off and only John Snort can do that. As far as your public image goes, well, I've never heard of you or that newspaper and I've lived in New York all my life. So, now, that's settled."

She was one of those short bitch types. One of the snotty kids in the schoolyard who would run around to the other kids in the in-group and say, "Sophie's hair is just dripping with grease." You just wanted to slap her.

"Besides." She smiled her snotty smile. "Refusing to be represented by a man is sexist, it's the same as racist. It's a case of reverse discrimination and furthermore it's male-exclusionist."

Where did she get a word like that? I looked at the wall-to-wall carpeting, her tweed suit, leather briefcase, silver cigarette case and gold earrings.

"No," I said quietly.

"I must insist. I have already put in eight hours of work for you *pro bono* on this case. I didn't have to do it but I did. I think you had better consider that because you are sounding ungrateful and irrational."

She picked up the princess phone and started to dial. I flipped through some copies of *Office Decorator*. She covered the receiver with her hand and hissed at me, "I have John Snort on the phone. I told him what your attitude is and he is very hurt. He's near tears. You call yourself a feminist but you don't mind brutally hurting the feelings of a very expensive lawyer who's trying to help you. He told me that he's never been so insulted in all his life. He also said that he refuses to represent anyone who claims they are being forced to be represented by him and if you don't say that you want him to represent you, he and I will walk off this case and you will walk into court twenty minutes from now with no lawyer."

She smiled.

"Now, before I forget, here is my bill for expenses incurred so far. Let's see. Three hundred for computer time, seventy for cab fare . . ."

We left together for court, still arguing in the cab. "Look Susan, I'm not a mean person, but if you do not listen to me and my expertise, you will lose. I don't mean to pressure you but I have to. It may sound unethical to you but it's ethical to me."

I wondered if ethical was anything like principled.

CHAPTER TWENTY-FIVE

When we got to Foley Square, the press was waiting but no John Snort. He was too hurt. June went to prepare and I looked over the motley crew. I recognized some of the guys from other cases I had covered, which believe me, did not bring any great comfort.

"Hey Sophie, really got yourself fucked in the ass this time ha-ha," called out the balding guy from ABC. Great. Most of them are revolting. They get sent from one story to another without any preparation or continuity and assume that everyone's guilty or else they wouldn't have been arrested.

"How come there's so much press?" I asked. "Did someone put this case in the UPI day book?"

"Naw," said the cameraman from CBS, cigar juice running down his second chin. "We're all here for the really big news of the day. Someone in the Westchester D.A.'s office was accused of moving stolen goods but the poor schnook dropped dead before he could get to court. So when we heard something was happening concerning that Commie lezzie case, we decided, what the hell, might as well bring in something so the station don't go sending us all over New York getting human interest location shots for a story on the weather."

June and I climbed to the top of the stairs while the

cameramen jockeyed for position. There was something about wearing a dress, the wind blowing through my short hair, my earrings glittering in the cold sun, that let me feel strong. This was, after all, my moment of glory. This was the switch from reporting news to making it. All over the country young girls would be looking up to me as an example of courage, independence and well, principle. Just like I had looked up to Germaine Covington years before. Like hundreds of defendants before me, I read my statement in a cool, crisp inspiring voice.

"I am a journalist with no political or criminal involvement in this case. I am refusing to give testimony to the Grand Jury because I believe it violates my First Amendment rights to freedom of the press. Second, I oppose the very existence of the Grand Jury because I believe that its process . . ."

The cameramen turned off their lights and started walking away. Only the radio and print press remained.

". . . its process, in general, is a manipulation and an invasion into the lives of political people whose activities should be protected by the constitution."

It was a dignified statement, I knew that. It felt good to stand out with the buildings like razors against the blue autumn New York sky. We opened for questions.

"Why are you protecting criminals?" asked *The Daily News.*

"If you're not covering up for terrorists then why are you going to jail?" asked *The New York Post.*

I tried to explain how Grand Juries work. How they can subpoena anyone and ask them all kinds of questions unrelated to the case they are investigating. "They could ask me who lives in my building or who shops at Key Food. If I answer one question I have to answer all of them. Then, if you refuse to cooperate, they send you to jail for eighteen months without even charging you with a crime."

I was getting worried. This wasn't much fun at all. I mean, when the press conference was over they would go get a bacon, lettuce and tomato on white toast and I might be headed inside.

I hoped Evan remembered to water the plants. I hoped Chris was right, I could use a little of that white skin privilege. Was that a sick thing to think? I didn't know what I felt anymore.

We found John washing his face in the men's room. He filed some motions and argued some arguments and got the court date postponed one month. That evening I watched ABC news and saw reporters crowded around my father lying on our living room sofa, his finger still hanging out of his mouth.

"She's always been fascinated by terrorists," my mother said in her chatty, helpful way. After all, this was her big chance to be on TV.

"What about you Mister Horowitz? Do you support your daughter's involvement with militants?"

My dear old dad took his finger out of his mouth and looked into the camera, right at me.

"They should go to Russia." he said.

CHAPTER TWENTY-SIX

Feeling in need of a little sisterhood, I walked over to the offices of *Feminist News*. Those women had been there for me through thick and thin, and I had been there for them. Three years it's been since we first started the newspaper in Chris' living room. Now we have a circulation of seven thousand and distribute another thousand free to women in prison. My column was called *On the Right and Left*, which meant that I came under a lot of criticism from people, but my sisters always defended me. I remember once when I interviewed lesbian nuns and got bloody tampax sent to me in the mail. Another time I criticized a prominent male leftist for sexually harassing his students and lots of his friends wouldn't talk to me for a year. Last spring was the worst of all — the spring of the sado-masochism controversy. I covered a conference on lesbian sado-masochism organized by a group called The Sexual Outlaws. It was held at midnight in a large basement packed with women in studded collars and leather shirts, some with crew cuts, all looking like desperados.

"How many women here do S/M?" the MC asked.

About half raised their hands.

"This is a support meeting for sado-masochists. No one has permission to say anything negative about S/M. No one who doesn't do S/M has permission to speak at all."

They passed the microphone back and forth while women told their stories. One older woman, calmly dressed in sweatpants and a sweatshirt, took the floor.

"My name is Tina," she cooed. "I get off on creating a scene. Do you know what that is?"

No Tina, tell us.

"I create a fantasy involving you. You may not even know you're in it and once it starts you have no control over it." As she was telling the story, she started, ever so slowly, to unzip her sweatshirt and untie her sweatpants, until both dropped to the ground, revealing leather and chains draped across her torso and a silver dagger gleaming between her breasts. The outlaws oohed and aahed. I felt sort of nervous. Then, it hit me, so to speak, that she had just created an exhibitionist fantasy for herself and we were her unknowing and in my case, unwilling, partners. The women loved it. They cheered and clapped until their gaiety was broken by an angry voice from the back of the room.

"When you slept with Charisse in Northampton, you nearly killed her."

The murmurs of scandal rippled through the crowd.

Tina stood there proudly with her head held high, her iron and leather wrapped breasts thrust forward.

"Charisse never said stop."

I called my piece A Sexual Outlaw Is Not Necessarily A Revolutionary. It was long but it made the point for women who couldn't get past the first paragraph. I got hate mail for months and an anonymous can of Crisco but my sisters stood by me. Even though they didn't agree with me, they were right there, dependable and supportive. Gosh I love them so much.

At the office my sisters were in deep despair. They greeted my entrance with expressions of dark suspicion.

"Look who's here. Hey Bonnie, where's Clyde?"

After a few more minutes of succinct conversation the situation became clear.

"Look Sophie." Chris took me over by the window. "Paranoia is running high and wild among the feminists. Jackie thinks that Kathy is an agent and Gerri is checking Julia's references. We spent the morning accusing each other of being government infiltrators. Now we're breaking for lunch."

"What kind of community response have we gotten?"

"Well, as far as I can tell, no one is calling the office for fear that the phone is tapped. Advertisers are slipping notes under the door though, and then running away."

As we stood there a little slip of paper came floating in through the mail slot. We listened to the patter of army boots running down the hall. I picked it up.

Dear *Feminist News,* please cancel all accounts for Feminist Exterminating Company and please burn all records that we ever did business with you. Please eat this message.

"Sophie, you know as well as I that without that revenue we'll never be able to put out another issue. Sophie . . . ?"

Chris was looking at the floor. "Sophie, if you don't resign, temporarily of course, you know, a leave of absence, we're all going on permanent vacation."

I looked out the window at the two agents sitting in an old Oldsmobile. I knew I had no choice.

CHAPTER TWENTY-SEVEN

A pariah to my friends, with fifty-four dollars to my name, I was back pounding the pavement looking for work. I tried registering with temporary typing agencies but I didn't have the clothes to apply. My neighbor, Rick the Queen, claimed he could get me a gig in a restaurant downtown where some of his friends were enjoying stable employment. He came through for me, and by Monday evening I was walking to work at Yes Sir Mister President. My last waitressing job, the one at Brew and Burger, had ended when I tried organizing a Waitresses Collective with the slogan "Serving the Women Who Serve the World." The boss didn't care for it. Remembering Fran Marino and her animals, I walked into a dining room full of fat men in business suits.

The manager, Donnie, put me on the floor right away. "I'll just throw you in and see if you drown."

"Yes Sir Mister President?" I tried to smile but all I could do was raise my eyebrows. My first table ordered two Becks on tap.

As I poured the drinks, Donnie talked to me out of the corner of his mouth. "Serve your cherry with the beers, dear." So I put a cherry in each of the beers. What did I know? I figured they had to be regulars with weird tastes. I got a twenty dollar tip. Something was not right. Experience had taught me that the only people who really leave good tips are other waitresses, or people who want something out of you that you don't want to give them. I stopped one of the other girls. Her nameplate said Yes Sir Mister President My Name is JOANNE.

"Hey Joanne, those guys gave me a twenty dollar tip."

"Honey, you'll have to wait until Shelley's through, you're next. You'll have to use the elevator."

"For what?"

"To suck them off, what do you think?"

For one minute I actually considered it. I considered sucking on the penises of fat Wall Street animals for twenty dollars a shot. I've had friends who have done it. Linda, an old-fashioned bar dyke with a tattoo, put on a negligee and worked the reception desk for a whorehouse on East 27th Street. She had to say, "I have a lovely blonde for you. She likes sixty-nine, around the world and grecian urn. That's apartment 'P,' for pleasure." She made one hundred fifty dollars a day. Then there was Judy, who was in my women's group some years ago. She worked as a masseuse to get through college. She said that you had to keep up with the porn mags to know what men were going to want. She said that if on Monday *Hustler* had some story about how the brand new kinky way to get off was to come in a woman's hair, then by Tuesday afternoon every man wanted to come in your hair. She said that she could read men like stop signs. She knew them so well, she could see one walking down the street and know everything about what humiliating, painful and boring things he liked to do. It would really be interesting to know men that well. I walked into the manager's office.

"Donnie, I'm sorry, I can't work here."

"That's all right honey. This isn't for everybody."

I walked out the door and into the night, later realizing I still had the twenty dollars in my pocket. I wonder how long they waited in the elevator.

CHAPTER TWENTY-EIGHT

I was worried about money. Really worried. I didn't mind living on potatoes — in fact, I preferred living on potatoes. But the bills were piling up and resources were running out. On top of it I was getting depressed. I couldn't go anywhere, I couldn't do anything. I needed a way out. What would make a lot of money fast? Drugs didn't make sense with all this police trouble and besides, it was a field with a lot of competition. And then it fell calmly upon me like a beam of sunlight. Pornography. I could write pornography. It wasn't so bad. It wouldn't be too hard. I had a pornographic mind, at least that's what my mother says. I could write pornography for lesbians. Start a whole new market. This could be the beginning of something really big. I'd get famous and appear on the David Susskind show wearing a ski mask. The Lesbian Pornographer. It felt possible.

I went to my typewriter and began to get nervous. Usually I start hitting the keys before I even sit down, typing furiously like Little Richard at the piano. It was going to be harder than I thought, there were so many complications. First, it couldn't sound like regular dirty, sleazy porn. "He thrust his throbbing cock into her juicy cunt." That just wouldn't do it. Most nouns, verbs and adjectives were unusable. I couldn't bring myself to write words like "stroke," "wet," or "hungry." They're meaningless. Also, I certainly didn't want to make an unnecessary contribution to the world of things that men jerk off to. I wanted it to be meaningless to men and wonderful for women. But, that wouldn't be too hard, women can jerk off to the bible. I, for example, masturbate to *The New York Times*. The main thing was that I wanted it to be real. I wanted it to describe sex the way women really have it. The real thing is usually a combination of thrill and frustration, comfort and conflict. It's basically very delicious but surely more complicated than the gothics or paperbacks would have you believe.

I sat back with my feet up on the desk and took a hit off a cigarette. What was sex like with Lillian, or any woman? When does it start and stop? Sometimes it starts over dinner or before, when you're chopping and smelling and sauteing the food. It's funny with women, the illusions and fantasies don't come so much from TV or Mom or eighth grade English. It's a special combination of what each woman brings to bed with her, her own courage or fear, her own private passions. I like the heavy physicality, touching and being touched in the same way, feeling the folds and wrinkles of her vulva, feeling mine being enjoyed in the same way. One woman called it "Writing graffiti on vaginal walls." It's a great urban metaphor. And there's also the thrill, every time, of knowing that everything in the world tried to stop this woman next to you in bed from being there, but she got through anyway, only because she wanted to and had decided to. All these feelings were what I wanted to synthesize into my pornography. I narrowed it down to one scene, to one seduction, to one moment of rising breasts with their red flush, to one minute of one tongue on my cunt, one minute of coming and kissing the mouth that made you come from tongue to tongue. None of the words were right.

I tore the paper out of the machine and tried again. It all came easier this time. I typed for two hours straight until I had a nice short story, good enough for any stroke book, called *Cycle Suck*, about two motorcycle men and their sailor boy. It should be good for fifty dollars.

Lillian and I talked on the phone the next morning.

"Don't you think it's a little unethical to write gay male pornography when you've never been a gay man?"

"Well, I've slept with one."

"Sophie, don't rationalize. If you're going to exploit gay men for money, that's okay, but you have to be honest about what you're doing."

I decided to sell it now and think about it later. Or maybe I could go back to restaurant work.

CHAPTER TWENTY-NINE

Two days later, after a series of humiliating interviews, I started to work at the Great American Health Food Bar by City Hall. Secretaries with painted faces and fingernails came in on their half-hour lunch breaks to order glorified fast food like curried tofu on pita bread with yogurt, brewer's yeast and a coke. The staff was composed of five lesbians, two Italian boys — one with an Andy Capp tattoo and one with Jesus on the cross — and a student at the Union Theological Seminary who was about to be married. I couldn't help but feel bad. Every time one of those secretaries spent her hard earned money on alfalfa sprouts on toasted seven-grain bread, cottage cheese with granola and a coke, and the bill came to seven-fifty, I felt bad. I felt so bad that I couldn't bring myself to remember that she had four items instead of three. At the end of the third day the boss came up to me.

"You don't like it here."

"Yes I do Bernie, I love it here, I really do."

"You don't smile at the customers."

"Bernie, I really try, I really do. Sometimes I can't actually smile but I do raise my eyebrows, see?"

At the age of twenty-four, with no degree and a reputation to match, I was begging Bernie for a job that I didn't want.

Tears streaming down my face, I walked out into the autumn air in my leafy green apron and carrot top hat, and walked home slowly through the Lower Eastside. I really wanted to drown my sorrows in a fat kielbasa and mashed with sauerkraut and gravy, challah bread and a Tuborg dark, but I couldn't afford it. I really wanted to feel Lillian put her strong hands around my waist and roll me into bed or the tub. I really wanted to buy six different kinds of cheesecake and sit on all of them, squish ripe strawberries all over Lillian's body and squeeze a lime on her labia, slurping juice like oysters in their shell. But Lillian wouldn't be over for a few more hours and I needed something right away.

I walked into my apartment, surprising Evan. He was sitting in his usual place on the couch but this time he had a very guilty look on his face. Then I looked again. The coke! Evan was snorting lines from my cocaine. That was the last straw, that slimy pig. After all I'd done for him. Then I remembered I had better be cool. It had occurred to me, well actually, to Lillian, that it wasn't too hip to be doing all these illegal type things with Evan hanging around. Who knows how much he'd already picked up? Now, if I lost my temper, he'd have enough information against me that for fun or profit — or even worse, good citizenship — he could upset this entire ship of fools.

"How's the coke Evan?" I tried to sound friendly. It worked like a charm.

As soon as the drugs went up my nose I knew it was good quality. Two lines and I was really high. Soon I'd be wired and want to go running all over New York City talking to strangers on the street. I would separate myself from the city by leaning back and out of the picture, seeing it as one object, understanding its hugeness. But for now, it was important to just try and relax, enjoy the artificial clarity and see what came to mind.

Laura Wolfe came to mind. It was so weird, I'd thought

about her a lot since that first cocktail with Vivian in Soho. Poor kid. She'd come out at the wrong time and in the wrong place. No one would take a lesbian seriously then. There wasn't any support base for her. How frustrating it must have been to be so close to women like Vivian and have them be unwilling and unable to imagine being lovers with her. She had to watch them go through relationships with ego-tripping left honchos, and they probably came crying to her for advice.

What am I talking about? Here I am with Vivian in the exact same situation. That woman is ridiculous, you'd think she would have realized by now that all the privileges she's supposed to get from men haven't given her any of the things she wants most. I mean, I had the benefit of lesbian culture, a certain cynicism developed collectively — it protects me. But Laura had to face aversion therapy, I can't blame her for becoming a fucking sectarian. She needs those politics as a way of surviving in the world. It's not my way, but it's okay. If no one else takes her seriously, she still has the guts to take herself seriously. All right, too seriously, but I mean, it could have been me. That's what it all boils down to. All these years I deceived myself into thinking that if I had lived then, I would have been as bright and beautiful as Germaine Covington, but I forgot one thing. I would have been one dead dyke, I would have been Laura Wolfe.

Is that why I'm so attracted to Vivian? Carrying on in Laura's footsteps. Or maybe she just turns me on. If she's lived thirty-four years and never been to bed with a woman she's got to be pretty scared, it's got to mean a lot to her. From the way she talks about losing her friendship with Laura, it's clear she's got regrets. I guess there was a lot of love there. I'd sensed some deep sadness in Vivian. Some sense of loss, of disappointment, a layer of conflict. You could tell that she's a woman who has a private craziness. Who goes into her room alone and screams and cries and talks to herself and breaks things and doesn't clean them up and washes her face, puts on a dress and goes back out into the world for another round.

"This coke is good, real good." Evan sniffed.

I decided to do a few more lines. Lillian wouldn't really mind. How much more trouble could I get into? I decided not to answer that question. I took Neil Young off the stereo and put on Coltrane's *Ascension,* saw Evan wince.

He took the record off. "I can't listen to that stuff. How about *Bob Dylan's Greatest Hits Volume Two?*"

"No."

"Volume One?"

"No."

"Oh."

Wow, all I had to say to Evan was "No," like I was the boss or something and he'd listen. Why hadn't I ever thought of that before? God what a wimp.

"Let's compromise and play the radio," he suggested.

"Okay."

It was tuned to the public radio station.

"Welcome to the Feminist Men's hour. Brought to you by the Gentle Anti-Masculinist Men of Greater New York. Our slogan is 'It's okay.' Today we're going to be taking calls from other feminist men so that we can be the world's first on-the-air gentle men's support group. Here's a call now. Hello. You're on the air."

It all had to do with my mother.

It's okay.

I shut it off.

"Evan, let's do some more lines."

He laid them out with a razor blade. "Sophie, where did you get all this great coke? It hasn't even been stepped on once. It's the best I've ever tasted. I think it's pharmaceutical."

"Yeah it's really . . . what did you say it was?"

"Pharmaceutical."

"Pharmaceutical . . . pharmaceutical . . . where have I just heard . . . oh shit."

"What's the matter?"

Of course, Melonie Chaing. She had pharmaceutical coke and it tasted just like this. In fact, I'd bet my recipe box that it was this. How could I have been so stupid? I looked down at the coke spoon in my hand. Galileo's face was covered with white powder. Vivian Beck and her fucking Italian silverware. Germaine was right, I am a bad detective.

Well, they might have made a fool out of me once, but now I was going to turn the tables on them, those bums. Beck and Chaing were in cahoots somehow and the whole thing led to Seymour.

I ran into my room and looked at Seymour's phone bill. There it was goddammit, that Westchester number was Vivian's. You can't trust those girls, I should have known that. I needed to call that Beck bitch right away. Wait a minute, what the fuck good would that do? I wanted to confront her face-to-face. I had to be smart about this or I'd blow the whole show. There had to be a way.

CHAPTER THIRTY

Lillian came over straight from the station.

"Sophie, there are three FBI agents hanging around outside in front of your building trying to look inconspicuous. Blond boys from Utah wearing blue jeans, trying to fit in. The drug dealers are strutting around nervously thinking they're narcs."

"That's not all that's happening" I added glumly.

I told her everything that had been revealed in the last few hours while we cooked up some stuffed cabbage made with raisins and kosher wine, for that special sweetness. Soaking in the tub we laid out a plan. Lillian needed to create a diversion while I escaped and made my way to Vivian's.

Quietly, I smoked a Tarryton, chewing on the charcoal filter, watching Lillian sit in the bath. It was one of those moments when I could see her age. Her neck and hands were getting rougher, not smooth and pudgy like my own. She always acted like a kid, wearing crazy clothes and dyeing her hair all kinds of colors, bleaching her eyebrows and having a good time. But at some moments I could see her getting tired.

Lillian's smart. She's beautiful and courageous but willing to live a quiet minor life. Her friends, her cup of coffee, are enough for her. She doesn't have ambition. She doesn't mind working in the rape crisis center weekend after weekend and then getting up every day to work in the same office until five o'clock when she staggers home, tired. She doesn't mind adding a bit of jolliness and comfort to other people's adventures but she never wants to be the center of things.

"Lillian are you sure you can handle it?" I regretted it the moment the words finished coming out of my coarse mouth.

"Sophie, don't you have any faith in me at all? Sometimes I think you really underestimate me. You act like I'm boring or something. Just because I'm not as glory hungry as you . . ."

"Lillian, relax."

"That's not fair. First you insult me and then when I get mad you try to smooth things over. It's not right. You have to let me get angry and not be so afraid of it. I'll show you what it's like to be bored — you're so worried about expending any of your valuable energy on mundane trivial topics like other people's feelings. How's this? I'm going to talk about that forbidden subject, what I did today. Today I did my laundry. I separated the whites and the colors . . ."

"Lillian, do you have to get hysterical? Is this necessary?"

"I used extra-strength bleach to get out those tough stains. Then I combed my hair. Then I bought a pack of gum. Juicy Fruit, I like it better than Doublemint." She was running out of steam.

We dressed silently. I knew I was supposed to feel bad but I didn't. Lillian is really a great person and she does take a lot of shit from me, but I'm just not interested in discussing our relationship. I let her talk — wait for her to finish and move on to the next topic. Talks like that can go on forever, like sports broadcasters, the same old stuff over and over again, you can't tell one game from another.

In the meantime the hours disappear and nothing interesting has happened.

She went down to the corner pay phone like we planned. The idea was for her to look guilty, act like she was paranoid, but didn't notice the agents. Then she was to call Information.

"May I have the number of the Armed Struggle Violent Revolutionary Council? Yes that's A-R-M-E-D as in bearing arms. Thank you."

It worked like a charm. The way she described it later, the agents all moved from the stoop to the corner booth, leaning conspicuously on the garbage can.

The drug dealers were losing patience. "You guys narcs or what?" they asked. " 'Cause we don't need you guys just hanging out like you belong here, you are not fooling anyone, do you hear me? Why don't you just do something already instead of just hanging out, hanging out. Shit — it's annoying, man."

I hung out the bedroom window and dropped onto the fire escape. Climbing up the ladder I looked out onto the rooftops of the Lower Eastside. It looked just the way it did when my grandparents came over in 1906, except for the housing projects of course. The twentieth century stood out in the background. All those massive glass boxes full of women typing and xeroxing and programming. Soon my neighborhood would be gone, leveled by greedy developers and turned into luxury duplex high rises and condos. Young professionals, children of the white flight, were moving back into the city. The same city they spent their childhoods being afraid of. Hanging on to each other when they saw the Nutcracker Suite at a Christmas class trip. They were moving in with brutal rapidity. The drug dealers on the corner serve as the last stand between us and total homogeneity. I hoisted myself up onto the roof, stepped into the fire escape and made my way down into the neighbor's backyard, over the fence, and through the Polish sausage store to freedom.

CHAPTER THIRTY-ONE

In the train up to White Plains I thought more about the sequence of events. Melonie had offered to help me without me asking for anything. She connected me to Vivian Beck who had been real nice and helpful as well. Henry too, even though Mrs. Noseworthy thinks his story is screwy. But that day in the park, Vivian had acted like she barely knew Seymour. Yet her coke spoon and Melonie's coke were in his house and he'd called her on the telephone.

So I was being set up, that much was unfortunately clear. What could they possibly want from me, a nobody? Well, it was time to set them up. I had to go sweet-talk Vivian. If I really concentrated and used all my charm maybe I could find out what she knew. Anyway, I'd detected a certain hesitancy in her. Maybe she was having a change of heart? I called her from the station.

"Yes."

"Vivian?"

"Yes?"

"Vivian, this is Sophie Horowitz."

"Sophie, how nice to hear from you."

"It's nice to hear you too Vivian. You know I really enjoyed the time we've spent together and I appreciate how open and helpful you've been in sharing your memories with me. Coincidentally, I happen to be up in

White Plains for a story I'm doing on autumn leaves and I was wondering if I could stop by for a few minutes to see those photos you've told me about."

"Well . . ."

"It would save you the trouble of bringing them to me in the city. I know how busy you must be."

"Well, all right, if it's only for an hour."

"I'll be right there."

Great. Now how was I going to get over to her place? I had no money for a cab. I didn't even have enough money to take the train home. But, I was running on pure revenge and I knew it would get me through. I went up to a young blonde woman who got off the train with me. She was stepping into her car.

"Excuse me, I know this sounds strange, but I've come to visit a friend and I seem to have forgotten my wallet. You aren't going anywhere near Hartsdale Avenue are you? Could you just give me a lift?"

"Of course honey, get right in, I'm always glad to help out a stranger."

Uh-oh, a weirdo. I got in the light blue Pontiac and found out I was right. The dashboard was covered with little stickers saying *I believe in Him, Honk if you Believe in Jesus, Honk if you Believe in Elvis,* and *Jesus was Once a Fetus.*

"My name is Sophie."

"I'm Kathleen."

"Pleased to meet you. I was just noticing your stickers here."

"Aren't they nice? I'm vice-president of Westchester Right-to-Life."

This could be interesting . . . then again . . .

"I'm just coming back from a meeting in New York City," Kathleen said. "We're preparing for Saturday's activities. We stand outside of those horrible abortion clinics with photos of those poor dead, unborn babies. We do sidewalk counseling, trying to convince those desperate, miserable women not to kill their babies."

"What do you say to them?" I asked, sitting back in her blue velour bucket seat.

"Oh, we usually tell them that their baby is a God-given human being, that only God has the right to take away that life, that their baby might grow up to be a priest. Every day that we go there we save one or two babies."

I wanted to light a cigarette but I knew better.

"There are some weapons I always have to have with me. First, a seven by five billboard of an aborted unborn child. It costs twenty two ninety-five. I fold it up and carry it with me wherever I go. Then I have a twelve-week-old fetus in a jar. I had it on my desk for four days, but that poor precious unborn baby boy ... now I keep him in my car."

I sniffed the air, checking for formaldehyde.

"Also the Lord gave me a free xerox machine. I prayed and I got one."

"Have you ever been politically active before, Kathleen?"

"No, but nothing has ever been this horrible before. You know, abortion is far worse than what the Nazis did as far as I'm concerned. The unborn are more helpless. It was the fact that abortion was legal in Germany in the twenties that made Nazism acceptable. It's fascinating, the things one learns as a crusader in God's army."

"Yes, fascinating."

"Well, my dear, here's the address. Remember, there's the east way, the west way, the north way and the south way but the one way is the Lord's way, Amen."

"Amen."

She drove away, abandoning me in Suburbia.

CHAPTER THIRTY-TWO

The street was dark and cold as the wind blew across empty yards. It had been a long time since I was last in the country. Well, it wasn't really the country but there were more trees than people so it wasn't a place where I belonged. It made me nervous, all those trees moving this way and that.

I rang the doorbell. Vivian answered. She looked really bad, like she'd been crying and smoking too much.

"Hello?"

She had been drinking too.

"Vivian, what's the matter, you look very upset." Her skin was pale and chalky, beads of cold sweat on her brow.

We walked into the living room and sat down. My eyes immediately caught an old Dutch hutch filled to the brim with souvenir spoons. There were examples from Disneyland to Disneyworld and all the area in between. The international collection was sitting on an oak bookcase.

"Vivian, sit down next to me and tell me what's wrong."

"It's stupid."

"No, it's not, you look really upset."

"I'm confronting all the self-deception I've burdened myself with for the last twenty years and I have to accept that it's my fault. No one did this to me. I did this to myself."

"It sounds like you're feeling out of control." Straight women always feel out of control.

"Yes, I think that has a lot to do with it."

So far so good.

We talked for a while longer while Vivian poured cognac into souvenir snifters from the Knoxville World's Fair. "It's my boyfriend. I don't know what to do about him. There are some pretty wonderful things about him and then there are some pretty awful things about him. If only I could be beautiful, charming, witty and passionate all the time, he would be a lot more interesting."

"Vivian, that sounds a little off."

"Yeah it does."

I lit one of her cigarettes, Marlboro Lights, just like Lillian, but that's where the resemblance ended.

"Sometimes I think my life with men is such a pitiful stereotype. Sophie, why don't you like men?"

"Well, I wouldn't exactly put it that way. I like some men, my brother, the drag queen down the hall. But you know, I'm never close enough to any of them for them to be able to do anything to me, except those obnoxious types on the street. I guess I'm a little out of touch. One thing for sure is that I don't like the way they run the world, and I don't like the way their world intrudes into mine."

"I don't know Sophie, thinking about my relationships makes me feel like a cartoon character."

"What happened to your other husband, the one you married after Jerry got into Scientology?"

"Yeah, you know he sells video games now? I just found that out. Well, Daniel, that was his name. I met him in graduate school in Philly. He was one of those gentle men, you know, strong enough to be tender?"

"I've met the type."

She was feeling better now. I could tell. She just needed someone who would listen to her.

"Well, he read all these books on feminism, making love with him was different than other men. He seemed to be really interested in how my body worked. With the others I always felt that they were fiddling with me, like tuning up a car. Yet, at the same time, I had this forboding sense that he wasn't getting much out of it except achievement, that being a good lover was more of a burden than a thrill. We married in 'seventy-six and I accepted a teaching/doctoral student package at Columbia in Italian Lang and Lit. We moved back to the city and started making friends with other old radicals who had found themselves wandering through the deserts of academia. I joined a Marxist-Feminist study group."

"Why Marxist-Feminist?"

"Well, you know, when I was in the New Left I never made a decision for myself. Either Jerry or Laura told me what to think. But on my own, actually with some other women in the same pitiful predicament, I started getting my politics together."

"So, what did you decide? Come on Vivian, I want to hear the word."

She took a deep breath. "Well, feminism is clearly a-historical and insufficiently materialist but Marxism has an inadequate analysis of gender relations. I even wrote an article for a theoretical journal in which I stated that women's relationship to the mode of production is determined by her relationship to reproduction."

I scowled. "Vivian."

"Well, it can't be all feelings, there's got to be some science."

"Yeah, but it can't be all formula either, it's like Bach without sound, it's all math."

"Well, I lost interest soon anyway."

That Vivian — a bundle of contradictions. Sometimes I saw her as this feeling, open woman, other times as such a jerk. "So what about Daniel?"

"Daniel told me that he was gay and had contracted a case of venereal warts. I went without sex for two years. But I did finish my dissertation and published my book and spent more time alone in my apartment. I started an intricate and organized filing system for newspaper clippings and seriously developed my collection of souvenir spoons. Then I started teaching at Hunter. My life was getting stabilized. I went to the movies, I built my own life as one solid unit. Any relationship was an invasion, but I knew I needed relationships because I liked having other people who I could tell what I was doing. Then I got involved with the chairman of the department. I spent a lot of time in the lobby of his building pretending I was invisible whenever he would step out of the elevator accompanied by his wife, you know, when I was expecting to spend that time with him. Afterwards he would call me up and say how much he wanted to fuck me."

"What did you do?"

"I made friends with the doorman. One night we went out for a drink. Then we went to bed together. He wanted to move in. When my sister's husband got transferred to Idaho, they offered me a house to sit for a year while they tried it out. So here we are."

"You and your doorman."

"Sort of a post-modern romanticism, don't you think?"

The cognac was making me nervous. "Vivian, let's look at those pictures."

She brightened up and pulled an old album from the shelves. "This is me and Laura at a demonstration in Washington Square Park. Look, we're both wearing flowers in our hair. The woman over there turned out to be a police agent. The other woman in the back, she was killed by the National Guard."

"You two have certainly been through a lot together haven't you?"

"We certainly have. Even when we're not together, sometimes I think that so much of what I've gone through alone has something to do with Laura. Sometimes when it feels like a dream, I try to figure it out. Then I realize it's too complicated to understand. That's how I know it's real life. You know, I've always been a little paranoid. Never really trusted that people who were nice to me really liked me, I always thought they were after something else. After a while I got used to feeling that way. I decided it was just part of the package of being a neurotic woman in her thirties. Then, two years ago I got my FBI file under the Freedom of Information Act. I found out that the last year Laura and I lived together we were followed every day by agents. Can you imagine that? No wonder we both had nervous breakdowns. That kind of surveillance creeps in under your skin. That whole period was such an unnatural thing to live through. I don't know if any of us have really recovered. I don't know if we really want to."

"I didn't know you had a breakdown too. The same time as Laura?"

"Yes, right after I got married."

"It sounds like you and Laura have a rather intense connection."

"I guess you could say that. You could think that." She poured herself some cognac. "You can think whatever you want to think, Sophie, about me being repressed or permanently in the closet. I think you have this thin but solid layer of contempt for me. Heterosexuality hasn't delivered on any of its promises to me, but I *have* been straight all this time and there has to be a reason. Either I'm pitifully repressed or I really am straight. You know Sophie, I've never even kissed a woman. Can you imagine?

Oh I've come close, very close over the years, but at the last moment I could just never go through with it. I think I knew it would take all my courage for that first step, and that it would only be a first step. I once tried to make a list of how many steps there were to go through before you are actually lovers with a woman and I realized I didn't have enough stamina to make it through all of them."

The cigarettes were empty but I had to have one. I took out some rolling papers and started unwrapping the butts. "Well, what are the pros and cons for you?"

"Well, the pro would be that I'd like to be in a relationship with someone who was nice to me. That's a revealing fantasy isn't it? I guess I still hold some fairy tale view of women together. It's so strange, you know, in the early seventies, one day, half the women's movement came out as lesbians. It was like we were all sitting around and the ice cream truck came and all of a sudden I looked around and everyone ran out for ice cream."

"Everyone but you."

"I didn't know where they had all gone. Oh lots of those women are straight again, but at least their sexuality gives them some sense of movement . . ."

"And the cons?"

"Well, I guess my major con would be that I would freak out in the middle and really not want to be there, or worse, that I would like it so much I'd never go back and my whole world would be turned upside down."

"That's a con?"

"I mean, it's embarrassing, Sophie. I'm scared that I don't know how to make love to a woman. I wouldn't know how many fingers to use when or what rhythm, or how to tell if she really liked it. It's embarrassing for me. I'm used to being competent. I mean, I wrote my dissertation didn't I?"

I smoked my precious cigarette. "Well, there's ways to be involved with a woman, Vivian, that takes all these fears into account. I mean, you could do it in stages. You know, set limits for your time together so that you know exactly what you'll be dealing with and then it would be up to you to decide when to move on to the next stage. So you could really enjoy a woman's breasts without being worried that you're going to get in deeper, over your head so to speak."

We both blushed. "That way you'd have some control and responsibility and wouldn't be doing anything you didn't want to do."

I could see her thinking it over. It did make good sense. I silently patted myself on the back. We were quiet. For one moment we looked each other full in the eyes. I saw what she really looked like. Sort of beautiful and hideous and vulnerable, her teenage acne scars showing through. I was glad she wasn't wearing any lipstick.

"So Sophie, what would the first step be?"

This was my moment. I had to play those cards.

"Well, we could lie down together and be close."

"That doesn't sound too good. I think I might start giggling." She was negotiating.

"Well, then we could just kiss, which would be really nice because I'd really like to kiss you."

"Yeah I'd like to kiss you too."

I thought I was going to die. It was so intense. We sat there for a moment. She turned her head to mine and then backed away.

"Vivian, would you like to kiss me?"

"Don't push me okay?" She was tense. "Just let me be. Just let me sit with it. Let me be the aggressor, I'd like that better. Just let me do it."

I waited and waited. Shit, I thought. I really blew it. Now I had to get out of the house with my integrity intact.

Then she leaned over and we kissed just like two women. Cheek to cheek, bites and licks, lips melting into each other. It was wonderful.

"It's wonderful," she said.

When her arms were around my neck and her body was pressed closely to mine, I reached into my pocket and, with one hand on her waist, said, "Vivian, is this yours?" holding up the silver coke spoon.

CHAPTER THIRTY-THREE

We drove along in Vivian's Volkswagen bug. It was about two in the morning.

"Where are we going, Vivian?"

"I don't know. I'm just driving."

"Where can you go in Westchester when you need to talk in the middle of the night?"

"I don't know."

So I'd played my card and now Vivian was pretty shook up about it. I didn't feel much like a smart guy hero. I didn't know what she was going to do, but I had the sense she didn't know either. We'd been driving around the burbs for some time.

"I need some gas." We pulled into a service station on the fringe of a large shopping mall. "Could you hand me my wallet? It's in the glove compartment."

"Sure." I opened it to a picture of a rather mean, unpleasant looking man with a short haircut. I couldn't see that well in the gas station light, but he seemed to be wearing army fatigues. Something about him was uncomfortably familiar. "Who's that?"

"My old man. He's a mercenary. That picture's from when he was in the Green Berets."

"You're shitting me. Vivian, you're full of surprises aren't you?"

"Yeah, I make one mistake after another. I don't even know how I got in this relationship. Look Sophie, I know you think I'm some dirty double-crossing manipulating bitch, but I'm really not. I just don't have the energy to explain everything to you now. Who are you anyway? Where did you come from? I didn't know you from the moon and all of a sudden I owe you all these explanations. How do I know you're not a cop?"

"Don't give me that bullshit."

She signed her credit card slip and we drove on.

The lights were on at the mall. Cars were cruising in the parking lot. Kids were hanging out smoking pot and drinking bottles of Boone's Farm Strawberry Wine.

"Why all the action?"

"It's Christmas shopping season. The town council decided to keep the place open twenty-four hours this year as an experiment. It creates jobs."

"Yeah, I bet."

She parked by the side of the Rite Aid Discount Drug Store and turned on the radio.

"So tell me more about your hulk. Is he still opening doors for adulturous university professors?"

"He's saving up his money. He wants to go to Angola." She looked stoned.

"Wait here Sophie, I'll be right back."

I thought about saying something like, "Okay but don't try any funny stuff," but decided against it. Vivian already had too much cops and robbers in her life. "Hey remember to get some cigarettes," I yelled out the window.

"What brand?"

"It doesn't matter."

I watched the kids dancing and drinking and having a good time. Poor kids, growing up in the suburbs must be so goddamn boring. Either you spend your life in "extra-curricular activities" or you're a greaser, wasting your brains on scuzzy rock and roll and bad drugs. Unless you're rich. Then you go to business school, grab a condo in the East Village, buy our Gussie's Pickles and open a wine bar.

"Here, I got you Lucky Strikes. Should put some hair on your chest."

"Very funny."

I couldn't tell if Vivian and I were fighting or what. I was waiting for information. She was waiting for morning. She took a bottle out of a Rite Aid bag and swallowed three pills very quickly.

"Vivian, what's that?"

"It's for my nerves, they're prescription. I'm a little stressed out right now and I don't want to get depressed or else I'll just crash, bottom out all over you and it won't be pleasant. I just want to get my head clear."

"Yeah, but three? Isn't that a little much? Vivian I hope you're not considering suicide in Westchester as the final solution to this little problem we're having. Soon it'll all be over. You'll see. A few years from now, you'll be able to look back on this night and understand it. It'll be a fond memory."

"Sophie, never in my life has a single moment ever come when I've looked back at times like this with anything but questions. Disturbing, depressing questions."

She started the motor. We drove past Scarsdale High as the football team was just starting early morning warm-up. The sun was rising over the goal post.

"Sophie, I'm going to be sick."

She pulled over and stopped the car. As soon as the door swung open, a stream of vomit poured out of Vivian's mouth. I let her vomit it all out. I put my arms around her. She felt so thin and tired. I kissed her hair and whispered into her neck that everything would be all right. I wiped her face with my shirt and she buried her head into my breasts and cried until we both fell asleep.

CHAPTER THIRTY-FOUR

I heard Vivian sit up and start the motor but I didn't feel like opening my eyes. Kids were screaming in the school yard and the sun felt warm on my face. It was one of those mornings. Like when you've been driving all night just to get across Nebraska and when the sun comes up you find out you still have Iowa to go. No point in getting excited.

By the time I started stretching and looking around we were turning onto Hartsdale Avenue. There seemed to be an awful lot of cars parked on the street for a quiet suburb. A lot of cars, including police cars. When we pulled up in front of the house, a whole crowd had gathered in Vivian's yard. They were gawking and stepping all over the bushes. Policemen in uniforms and plainclothes were writing things in little note pads. We slowly got out of the car and walked up to the front door.

"This is my home. What is the trouble officer?"

Then I saw her. I almost swallowed my tongue. Eva, the true love of my teenaged years, that bitch. But there she was in her tweed suit and leather pumps. The man standing next to her was tall and tan. She strode over briskly, not batting an eye. The sun god spoke first.

"Miss Beck?"

"Yes?"

"I'm Peter Pope, the District Attorney for this area. Do you know this man?" He flashed a picture of Viv's doorman guerrila.

"Yes."

"I'm afraid Miss Beck that he is under arrest for murder."

"Oh."

Vivian wasn't surprised. I couldn't tell if she knew all along or had just gotten habituated to massive disappointment and heartbreak.

"Eva, take down this lady's name while I consult with Miss Beck." He walked Vivian away into the house.

So, after years of wonder, anger and fantasy, Eva and I were finally alone together again. She in her nylons and me in my vomit-stained shirt.

"Name?"

"Lanie Kazan."

"Occupation?"

"I sing at the Rainbow Room. Eva, what are you doing?"

"Relation to suspect?"

"We car-pool together."

"Sophie, I don't know what your problem is but you should not be here. You are under subpoena in a totally unrelated case. Now, if you're smart you will just get out of here and never talk to any of these people again. I'll give you one chance."

She looked me right in the eye. I remembered those baby blues with lightening streaks of yellow and green. "Just tell me," I said, "who did her old man rub out? Some political assassination? Was it a contract job? Did he use hand grenades or poison gas?"

She looked at me again. I remembered how pink her lips were. I remembered that they were the same color as her nipples.

"He killed a fairy."

She walked away.

"Thanks Eva," I said to myself. "Thanks for letting me off the hook."

I turned around to walk off into the crowd and stumbled right into Lillian and Mrs. Noseworthy. "Hi girls. Do you come here often?"

"Sophie." Lillian threw her arms around me, tears pouring down her cheeks. "How do you feel?"

"Like I'm coming down off an LSD trip. Lillian, Mrs. Noseworthy, what is going on here?"

"Sophie, get in my car and we'll tell you the whole story." Mrs. Noseworthy's grey hair looked beautiful against the yellow and red leaves. She pointed to a small foreign job.

"Mrs. Noseworthy, you drive a lavender BMW?"

"It makes me feel young."

"I bet."

We drove away from that sordid mess. I felt high from not eating but my imagination was dulled from over-use. I wanted to be there for Vivian but knew that I couldn't be. I just hoped she'd make it through so I could see her again. Something about seeing people at their worst usually makes me fond of them. Well, not all the time.

Lillian put her big arms around me and I settled back into her softness. "Okay Lil, give me the scoop."

CHAPTER THIRTY-FIVE

"You know Mrs. Noseworthy, my most consistent emotion during this case has been nausea. Do you think that's normal?"

"Well, Sophie, most detectives have little idiosyncrasies. Nero Wolfe never leaves his apartment, Spencer is a gourmet cook, King James hasn't slept with his wife in ten years and likes peppermint life savers. I'd say that nausea is a fine quality in a detective. Especially since making a business of snooping into other people's lives is a pretty disgusting way to pass your time."

My head was hurting.

"Are you really feeling bad Soph-a-loaf?" Lillian was unusually cheery.

"I'm starting to feel so bad I can't think of anything else to say."

"Sophie, if you can't think of anything to say, you must be dying." She chuckled. What was Lillian so titillated about?

"So, Lily, tell me the story already."

"Well, after you left I was pretty angry at you. I sat in that ugly apartment of yours with Evan and got upset. I was sitting by the window, crying, when the phone rang. It was the sweetest, most comforting voice — Mrs. Noseworthy. Did you know that she's King James? Why didn't you tell me? Well, she was so nice and invited me over for tea and we just talked about her books and your case. We went over all the facts."

Lillian smiled at Mrs. Noseworthy in the rearview mirror. "That's when we got to Mukul Garg."

"Mukul Garg?"

"Seymour's doorman. Remember him?"

A chill ran through my body. Something very unpleasant was about to fall right into my little lap.

"Well, just to find out some more about him, Mrs. Noseworthy and I went up to three-fifty Central Park West and spoke with the other employees in the building about him, and some of the tenants. One, this older man, a professor or some such, was most helpful. We found out that Mukul lived in White Plains and that, as a matter of fact, he lived in the very same house as —"

"Vivian Beck."

My head hit the roof.

"That's right Sophie, Vivian Beck's boyfriend was the doorman. But you must know all this by now, seeing as you've been to the scene of the crime."

"Uh, sure Mrs. Noseworthy, I figured it all out after a while."

"What clues gave it away to you?"

"Uh, intuition, I'm a great judge of character."

"Well, dear, when we realized you were unsuspectingly walking into a potentially explosive situation, I made an anonymous phone call to the police, in my best Italian accent. I thought it would be appropriate for the occasion."

"Sophie, you should have been there, she was just great. She tipped them off that Seymour's murderer would be found at the Westchester address. She's been to Italy and everything."

The Saturday afternoon traffic was picking up, the closer we got to the city. It'd been a long time since I'd done anything fun like go to a ballgame. Maybe I needed to take a day off. Play some chess, look at my stamp collection. Take in a museum. Hey, that might be a nice idea.

"I guess Vivian's implicated in the murder."

"Well, I thought so too, at first." Mrs. Noseworthy always seemed so even-tempered and clear. Maybe it comes with age. Probably not. "But since then I've been convinced to the contrary. We got out to Vivian's house early this morning, right before the police did. It takes them such a long time to do anything. This man has to check with that man who has to get permission from the other man. It precludes any imaginative spontaneity. Except when it comes to violence of course. At any rate, we sat in my car here in the early dawn having a rather pleasant chat."

"About the fauna of the Cape and how it compares to northern Michigan." I'd never seen Lillian so enthused.

"Yes it was quite pleasant. Then that Mister Pope and his associate drove up with four or five police cars. All full of fat balding men carrying guns. They surrounded the house and called for Mukul to surrender. He came to the window and looked out at a sea of police officers pointing guns at him. He was in his pajamas. I guess his soldier's sense told him it was not the moment to die a hero and so he attached a little white handkerchief to his electric toothbrush and waved it out the window."

We drove down Ninth Avenue. The horns were honking, the peddlers were peddling, the bums were panhandling. What a relief.

"By this time a crowd had gathered. As soon as he came out of the house Mukul started to cry. You know he looks like a gorilla but he really seemed to be quite soft inside. He said he knew his wife was having an affair with Seymour and when he realized what kind of sex Seymour was into, he couldn't stand the thought of Vivian as Epstein's . . . well . . . dominatrix. No, I don't think that's the word he used."

"Slut . . . he said slut."

"Yes, thank you Lillian."

"Oh God, the poor schnook," I said. "All along Vivian was selling coke to Seymour and her old man thought it was nookie-nookie and goes and kills the slob. Shit. God, what was Vivian doing with a guy like that? Everything else about her makes perfect sense. You could predict it. But this marine doorman with an Ehrlichman hair cut. I don't know."

"Oh Sophie . . . You shouldn't be so surprised really. It's part of the burden of heterosexuality. I'm sorry Mrs. Noseworthy . . ."

"That's all right Lillian, we're all entitled to our opinions."

"Thank you. So Soph, you know, they try and try to find a man who's different and all they get is false promises, deception and a passivity that passes for gentleness. They just can't stop. It's a compulsion. I guess Vivian just reached the point where she got involved with a man who made no pretenses about being different. He was honest about how much of an asshole he is and she was able to accurately assess exactly what she was and was not going to get out of it. Maybe it's not so disappointing that way."

We were walking up the six flights to my apartment. "Lily, I have a confession to make. I've been making a fool of myself over a straight woman."

"Not again."

"I'm afraid so."

"My poor baby. Let me run you a nice hot bath."

CHAPTER THIRTY-SIX

It was Monday afternoon. Melonie and I were having breakfast. Two shots of Jim Beam Sour Mash and a Molson wash. Melonie was coming off a gig looking fresh as a kumquat. She wore khaki parachute pants, a white shirt, a black leather jacket and a blue sparkle tie. She looked really sharp. I wore my pants and my shirt. I looked really tired.

"Okay Melonie. I want it straight from you this time. I hope I don't need to tell you how annoyed I am. Listen to me. I was almost implicated in a bizarre murder, came face-to-face with Public Enemy Number One, got subpoenaed by a Grand Jury and just missed running into a Da Nang alumnus while I was making out with his neurotic girlfriend. So now why don't you tell me the truth for a change. Hmmm?"

"Well, Sophie." She was cool as a cucumber in Montana in December. "I fronted that coke to Vivian when she told me what she had in mind. Helping Laura."

"Laura?" I ordered another round.

"Yeah. Vivian still sees herself as the only person in the world who really cares if Laura Wolfe lives or dies. She hasn't heard from her yet, but Vivian's counting on some message coming through sooner or later and she wanted to have a large sum of money waiting to help Laura get out of the country or whatever." Melonie took out a pack of Rothman

Internationals. The kind with the gold band.

"Hey Melonie, you want to know what the fuck I figured out all by my little stupid self?"

She didn't even raise an eyebrow, I got the feeling she was adopting her psychologist persona: Go ahead you little nothing, yell and scream and tell me everything. I'll write it all down in my book. I won't tell you a thing. Go ahead, I dare you.

"Yes?"

"It was you who told Germaine Covington that I went to Seymour's that night. Am I right? It had to be you. You're the only one with enough information to figure it out."

"Well, I don't know you intimately, it's true, but I am a good enough diagnostician to know that if you, Sophie, were borrowing leather it could only be for a story. Since I was familiar with Seymour's proclivities and your discussion with Henry, it all fit together very nicely until Seymour was murdered. Then I had a lot of questions."

"So did I."

"But mine have been answered."

She had a point there. "So Melonie, you have been in touch with Germaine all these years."

"Someone had to stand by her. She's a revolutionary you know." Melonie's eyes blazed. I recognized that look. That cold, blank look. I didn't want to know any more. The more information she gave me, the more trouble I was in. I tried to start wrapping up this discussion.

"Well Mel, it's been great talking to you but I have some clothes in the dryer and I think I left my typewriter on."

"Listen Sophie, I'm older than you and there are some things you don't know about, so pay attention. I grew up in Chinatown. I was the only one who spoke English so they used to bring me out at age six to translate when the man from the city came to inspect the family store. So I was smart and got sent to an all-white school for quote

intellectually gifted girls. There were five of us from Chinatown and we used to bring our lunches from home in cleaned-
out plastic containers and eat together every single day. We
thought we could do anything, for a while. I wanted to study
literature and write stories. But no, I was Chinese so I got
tracked into all the science classes. They pushed me into
honors biology and got me a scholarship to Barnard, another
all-white school that wanted me to smile and study hard
and spend the rest of my life in a laboratory. I managed to
convince them to let me go into psychology. I spent every
day working in the library so I could afford to keep working in the library. Then I met Henry."

She brushed her hair out of the beer. "He didn't know
Chinese but he knew he was Chinese. He wore a patch on
his jacket that said Yellow Power. That was an attitude I'd
never run into before. He took me around to meet his spoiled
angry friends who were throwing away their chance at a
good education. They all liked me, wanted me to be in their
groups, at their parties. Do you know why Sophie?"

Of course I knew why.

"Because I was a Third World Woman." She was shaking.
"Only one person didn't treat me that way. Germaine
Covington. She had more charisma than anyone I had ever
seen off a movie screen. She didn't tell me my studies were
bourgeois or that I shouldn't take a straight job in a straight
clinic. She was smarter than that. She wanted me to know
she had faith in me. She knew I had to come into changes
on my own, and that I would. She believed I would find my
own way. Then, when Germaine got into trouble, she came
to me. She came to me and I agreed to help her. I didn't
need to think about it. It was pure instinct. I was strong
enough to know what was right, and it invigorated me,
doing what was right, it gave me power. I'd work all day at
Payne Whitney connecting names to ridiculous categories
and watching psychology fuck people over. Then at night

I'd be getting credit card numbers and false identification cards. I felt a buzzing throughout my body. There was a hidden electrical wire running under my skin, burning, and only I could feel it. That wire's name was Germaine Covington." She looked me right in the eye.

"So how does Germaine connect to Seymour?"

"I'd been selling drugs to Seymour for a long time. I began to realize he had some illegal money sources and that the asshole couldn't keep a secret. He always was an asshole. Germaine blackmailed him on the basis of the information until he agreed to set up this robbery. At the same time Pope started to come under investigation and he needed an easy out. The three of them set up the whole thing. Pope got the records, Seymour gets the story and Germaine gets killed off."

"But Germaine wasn't really killed."

"No, but someone was. I don't know anything about that side of it. Pope set everything up."

With a little help from Henry, I thought to myself, and immediately changed the subject. "So what about Laura Wolfe?"

"I don't know. No one has seen her. I hear your interest in her goes beyond professionalism. I hear you're a little in love with her."

"Come on Melonie." I coughed and walked over to the juke box. We were in an old Polish bar on Seventh Street and First. Most of the songs were polkas but they did have a few golden oldies. I played Janis's *Get It While You Can*, and ordered another round.

"Don't try to bullshit me Sophie. You have excellent diversionary tactics."

"Look Melonie, if you think that psych stuff is bullshit then don't use it against me."

"It's bullshit but it's good for one thing. It gives the person who uses it power. And I'm interested in the gathering and maintenance of power. Henry says you have pictures of her all over your walls. He says you know every detail about her personal history. Forget about her Sophie. She doesn't even know you're alive."

Physically high and spiritually low, I stumbled home past the dealers, the bums, the Polish women getting their hair done, the Puerto Rican men listening to Tito Puente, the gentrifiers buying quiche. After an arduous climb up the stairs I collapsed in my apartment. I thought about giving up drinking. I'd taken it up for effect and now it was starting to have an effect. I had to get my head straight or at least clear. The fact that Henry, Melonie and Vivian were acting on their political convictions and personal relationships didn't take away that they lied to me, and that hurt. God those connections were strong. Vivian had barely spoken to Laura in ten years but was willing to risk everything for her. They'd become each other's art. It was interesting but I still felt embarrassed, like a little kid who just realized that she wasn't really invited to her parents' cocktail party. Or planning to meet a woman somewhere and having her show up with her boyfriend. Little subtle messages that tell you you're nothing. I started eating some cold potato kugel.

The story was almost over. Soon I'd have to sit down and write it. There's a certain relief when that moment comes. I'd lived with these people and this information and now that time was almost up. I could say goodbye to them.

Sometimes it's sad, but it's always scary. Maybe the magic won't come back, maybe another interesting event won't present itself. It makes me want to hold on for one more episode. I never know for sure if I'll again be able to find a story where no one else has seen one. That chance to sit in my apartment, typing and at the same time communicating with thousands of people without having to talk to anybody. Then, those golden moments of glory when a really good article appears and suddenly I have friends. Or the times when a poor excuse for journalism shows up under my byline and I don't hear from a soul for weeks. But good or bad, when each new issue hits the stands, everyone forgets forever about the ones that came before. It's a stark moment, that beat between stories, when I'm left alone with myself and the warm purring of my Smith-Corona.

Evan appeared with a backpack on his back.

"Evan, are you leaving my lovely home?"

"I'm going to Hawaii."

"Evan, how are you going to get to Hawaii? Swim?"

"I'm flying Pan Am. First Class. I made some money."

My coke. "What kind of money?"

"I've been watching you write at that typewriter. It didn't look hard. I'm pretty smart you know."

"So you've mentioned."

"So I wrote an article . . . for *Penthouse.* It's called *What Makes A Woman Good In Bed.* I got three thousand dollars for it. I'm going to Maui. I left some food in the refrigerator — ketchup and mustard. You can keep it."

I felt like I was sending my son off to Boy Scout camp. Maybe I could write an article for *Penthouse* called *What Makes A Woman Good In Bed* but maybe I needed to do a little more research.

CHAPTER THIRTY-SEVEN

It was a really good idea to take the day off. Originally I'd wanted to go to see the Yankees with Lou but he told me that the season was long over and besides, the Yankees had been out of contention for weeks before the Series. So, I ended up walking up Fifth Avenue, all bundled up in the beginning of winter attire, heading towards the Jewish Museum.

Before I learned that there were upper classes and lower classes I learned that there was uptown and downtown. The German Jews lived uptown and the Russian Jews lived downtown. Actually, by the time I was born this was no longer the case, but my grandmother forgot to mention that fact, so the Jewish Museum, overlooking Central Park, has always meant German Jews to me.

Most of their exhibits were usually about religious issues, artifacts ranging from pots to candlesticks or particular artists who happened to be Jewish. I like two topics: The Lower Eastside and certain aspects of the Holocaust, not the guilt and suffering part, but all the intrigues, the history and the infamous cast of characters.

There's a whole generation of Jews like me who are obsessed with the Holocaust the way other teenagers like Mick Jagger. We see each other embarrassingly slink in to see the four-hour version of *The Sorrow and the Pity* for the third time. We go to every exhibit, film or show about fascism and have hardcover editions of *The Rise and Fall of the Third Reich* sitting on our bookshelves. Lillian says that watching documentaries about Nazis with me is like watching the Academy Awards or the Superbowl with anybody else. I'm always saying "See, see that's Martin Bormann, he stayed in Hitler's bunker to the end and then split, Nuremberg sentenced him to death *in absentia.* Look, look, that's Ernst Roehm, he was gay, he got the axe in the night of a thousand swords." I know all the guys and their vital statistics. One thing I've noticed is that most exhibits, books, films, etc., focus on either the horror of the victims, or the horror of the victimizers. But the thing that's always interested me is that short quiet period of time, after the war, when Jewish women in Brownsville and the Bronx were hanging up their wash one day and a letter came telling them that their sister, mother, neighbor, friend, village, country had been exterminated. What did they say when they learned this? Did they speak to each other about it? What vows did they make? What did they resign themselves to? These are the questions I bring to the Jewish Museum. I don't ever see the answers. But I keep on going. I keep waiting for the exhibit on Jewish lesbians, I've got plenty of time.

I passed by exhibits on the Jews of Istanbul in the 18th century and took a look at Contemporary Jewish Painters. My eyes raced through the painting as if I were looking for a name in the phone book. There was nothing there that spoke to me. Wait. Over in the corner — now that was a familiar scene. A large, comfortable beat-up old armchair on a beat-up old rug. Next to it a magazine stand overflowed with copies of the *Forwards, Commentary* and *Hadassah News.* Facing the chair sat a big old TV from the forties covered with a doily, plastic flowers and bar mitzvah photos. It was home. I sat down in the chair. Automatically, the lights dimmed, the TV turned on.

An old woman in glasses and an apron appeared on the set and looked right at me. "What are you doing wearing that *shmata?* You're a *shanda* for the *goyim.* You should only get a good job and earn a living so you shouldn't be a *schnorrer.*"

The set turned off as the lights came back on. I looked at the name plate. The piece was called "Grandma." Now that's what I call good art.

I wandered around a bit more. I was pretty much alone except for this nun. Nuns, they make me nervous. Chrissie says most of them are lesbians anyway, but I don't know. I just don't trust them. Someone told me they're all married to Christ. That seems sort of out to lunch, you've gotta admit.

I stepped into another gallery, the nun came in after me. I went up the stairs. She glided after me. This was really weird. Was I being cruised by a nun? Is that possible? There was only one way to tell. I headed for the Ladies Room.

"I'm sorry, we're closing," interceded the guard.

"Oh yeah, sure, thanks." I stumbled out the front door. Well, if she wanted me that bad she could follow me into the park. It was six o'clock, there wouldn't be many people there.

When you tell someone you're from New York they usually ask two questions. "Do you ever go out?" and "Do you carry a gun?" The trick is that dusk in autumn is the best time to go into the park. The muggers haven't gotten used to the cold and you have one of those few opportunities to be alone, outside, in New York City. Besides, the greyness is eerie, like the moors in *Wuthering Heights.* It makes me feel like I'm in a fairy tale.

I looked over my shoulder, yep, there she was, Sister Mary Heroin or whatever her name was. Goddammit, oops I didn't mean to say that. Maybe she wanted to ask me for a donation.

I walked a little farther. We passed the Alice in Wonderland statue by the sailboat pond. That's where the fifty-year-old Irish maids hang out together with their little rich kids. We passed the 68th Street entrance, that's where the twenty-year-old Black maids from the islands hang out with their little rich kids and with their rasta boyfriends. I passed the children's zoo and walked under the tunnel just in time for the clock to strike 6:30. The zoo was completely deserted. I sat down on the bench opposite the empty seal pond and watched the little concrete figures dance around the clock singing *Silver Bells.* You can't get heat in your apartment, the subway never comes on time, but come November 1st you know that goddamn clock is going to play *Silver Bells.*

I lit a Kent Golden Light 100 and took turns switching smoking hands so my fingers wouldn't freeze and fall off. Yep, there she was again. She was a little nun, a young one. She sat down next to me.

"Hey Sis, what can I do for you?"

"My name is Laura Wolfe."

CHAPTER THIRTY-EIGHT

We sat in the bar at the Waldorf-Astoria. It was decorated according to a jungle theme. The mirrors had snakeskin trimming, the walls were covered in leopard skin. A blonde waitress in a safari shirt and tan hot pants came over to us.

"Would you care for a drink, Sister?"

"Oh no," she giggled piously, "I'll just have some orange juice please."

"I'll have a triple shot of rum, neat and a side of OJ."

"Here Sis." I poured half my drink into her glass. "You'll like this place, they serve macadamia nuts."

Laura Wolfe was calmer, softer, more serene than I remembered. Although, who knew what lurked under that exterior? She told me her story.

"I hadn't spoken to Germaine since she ducked out. She always treated me badly because I wasn't a big shot like her. But I didn't let her power-tripping get in the way. I put my personal feelings aside and supported her anyway, for ten years. It was the principled thing to do."

It occurred to me that I'd been spending a lot of time in bars lately. "Laura there's something I've been meaning to ask you for a long time. What is this principled-unprincipled thing? What does it all mean?"

She took a deep breath. "Principled is like honorable. It's when you put your personal ego and petty jealousies aside and do what is the objectively right thing, no matter how hard it is. You may lose a lot personally, but the revolution wins in the end. That's the contradiction, the commitment of the white middle-class American revolutionary. You are actively agitating for your own demise."

That Laura Wolfe. She has these bizarre ideas and they somehow seem to make sense.

"Laura, I don't know what it is but something about your perspective, although it has many fine ideological points, seems hard for me. It seems a little dehumanized."

"Well, what's your program?"

"What?"

"What's your program for making a revolution?"

"Well, I don't really have one. You mean like a ten-point how-to plan? No, I don't have one."

"Next question you need to ask yourself Sophie is what will society look like after the revolution?"

"Well, I don't know. I guess it depends on what people are into."

"No, that's how fascists come to power. We have to have a program that is both pre- and post-revolutionary in its vision. You, you call yourself a feminist. What does that mean?"

"Wait a minute Laura, I didn't go through all this shit to end up fighting about politics with you."

"Just answer my question."

"Well, I don't know really, it sort of means that people should be able to control their own lives and that we all have more options and open up our imaginations and try new ways of living and challenging . . . ."

"See, you have no program." She took a contented sip.

That Laura Wolfe. All my fantasies of reforming her were hopeless. I wanted to tell her that first of all, right now, there is no revolution. Second, when there will be one, if it's a good one, which is a big if, it won't be because people threw their humanity out the window. I knew then what I had to do.

"Wait right here I have to make a phone call. Chrissie is expecting to meet me at *Feminist News.* I don't want her to worry."

I smiled at the waitress and ordered another round on the way back to the table.

"So for ten years, not a peep." Laura continued. "Everyone else I knew had seen her or helped her in some way. Then, about three months ago I got a telephone call. She told me that she'd been watching me, that I was the real revolutionary, that I was in the Vanguard."

Oh, that word.

"You have to understand Sophie, all my life these women have been laughing at me behind my back and sometimes to my face. Like you and Chris. I know what you all think and say about me and it hurts, it hurts every single day, but I can't give in to that. It would be like trying to change myself to make friends with the popular girls. What's the point? So, when Germaine called and said that I was really radical, I believed her. When she invited me to join her new underground fighting cadre, I believed her. It was only when I got to the bank and realized what was going on that I understood I had been played for the fool. So here I am, thirty-four years old. My group disowned me, the police are looking for me. What's going to happen to my life?"

God, everyone I'd talked to lately was thirty-four years old. I made a mental note to get together with Lou as soon as possible. We could just listen to the Allman Brothers and not worry about things like this.

"What about your friends? What about Vivian?"

"Vivian? You know, I've been thinking about her a lot lately, after years of not thinking about her at all. Do you know her?"

"We've met."

"God, Vivian. It's been so long. We were really close, I was so in love with her. We used to sleep in the same bed together with our arms around each other but we never even kissed. Everyone around was coming out, but not Vivian. She was stuck in something and no matter how much love I gave her it wasn't enough. So you know what I mean?"

I had an idea.

"At first I thought it was just a question of being patient. I thought that there was real love and desire there and she knew it. But after a while I realized that she was holding me back. If Vivian couldn't face and validate her own feelings then she couldn't and that was it. It was sad but I had to leave her behind. I mean she couldn't stop herself from loving women, she just couldn't act on it."

"It must have been impossible for you in the student movement, Laura, it sounds so male and heterosexual. Yuch."

"Well, it was hard, I'm not going to claim otherwise but it made me strong too. I mean, I admit, I used to die a little every time my work was overlooked or when they wouldn't listen to me at meetings because I wasn't fucking anyone and I wasn't going to fuck anyone. But it was double-edged, you know, I really didn't want those men either, so I was glad that they didn't want me. When Vivian would come home crying after Jerry hurt her, I knew I would be able to put my arms around her and kiss her hair and whisper into her neck that everything would be all right. Then she would cry and we'd fall asleep like that. Those were our best moments together. But I was young then. Soon I learned that it isn't friendship that makes a revolution, it's comrades."

"When did you learn that?"

"Around 'sixty-nine or 'seventy."

"When you went to the hospital?"

She brushed her blonde hair back into her habit. "Oh, I get it, the investigative reporter does her homework."

"That's right." It didn't feel great.

Laura looked younger than Vivian. She was thin with bouncy ringlets and blue, blue eyes. Maybe it was because she dressed differently. I tried to remember how she used to look picketing all my events. No color coordination, no style, just clothes. Of course, she did look smashing in a nun's habit.

"Where did you get that get-up anyway?"

"Ripped it off from this shelter where I was staying, Sisters of Perpetual Bondage or something like that."

Hey, she had a sense of humor after all. One thing I noticed looking at all those pictures of her on my wall every day was that Laura Wolfe dressed a little bit like me.

"So what was that about, the hospital I mean?"

"It's pretty much what you can imagine. They strapped me down and showed me pictures of women pretending to make love to each other. Not real women, not real love, more like those boarding school pornography shots, the kind that men like. Then they gave me electric shock. At first I wondered why my friends didn't come and rescue me but then I remembered the pain of the Vitenamese and knew the doctors couldn't break me. I could live like them."

"So you formed Women of the Roots."

"Right, which then split over the question of Cuba into Some Women of the Roots and Women's Committee for the Roots. There's been a lot of change since then in the formations' efforts to build a mass base. You can't convene a revolution you know, it has to be slowly, painfully and precisely built."

I looked at the zebra skin clock. It was time to go. The check came.

"Hey Laura, guess how much orange juice costs at the Waldorf-Astoria?"

"I don't know."

"Five dollars, and it wasn't even freshly squeezed."

I signed the check. "That's room forty-eight," I told the busy cashier, and off we walked into mid-town Manhattan Monday night.

"Where do you want to go now?"

"I don't know Laura, let's just walk. Are you hungry? Maybe we can get something to eat."

We walked all the way down to the Saint Mark's Theatre. They were having a Faye Dunaway festival. *Chinatown* and *Mommie Dearest.*

As I expected, Vivian was standing under the pink marquee lights. When they saw each other the whole city lit up with the power of the hope in their faces.

I stood back a bit and let them talk and touch and look at each other. It was getting cold. God I love this neighborhood. Soon it would be overrun with sushi bars but right at the moment it seemed so much a part of me. There would always be something interesting happening here. If I was sad or lonely, all I had to do was walk outside and I could feel life wrap her arms around me and let me crawl into her.

Laura got into Vivian's Volkswagen leaving the two of us looking at each other across the sidewalk as punks and tourists and Ukranians hurried by between us.

"Vivian I . . ."

I didn't have the words to tell her what I felt. I was surprised by the sharp flash in my side, it was a precious and short moment. I wanted to hold on to it but I didn't know how.

"Sophie you used me and I used you. I know that. It doesn't matter what we think passed between us. Everything's too confused to figure out what part of it was real."

"No Vivian, please don't throw me away like that."

"Look, I'm sorry I have to tell you this but I do. Melonie and Henry are friends of Germaine's. They've been protecting her for a long time and they're not going to stop now. Do you understand? There's only one person who really knows what happened at the bank and that's Laura. Look Sophie, what I'm trying to say is that you've been set-up okay? I know you have a big ego and this is going to be hard for you to take but we fed you information because we wanted you to lead us to Laura and you were naive enough to take the bait. You believed that all this was naturally falling into your lap. Only now I want Laura for different reasons than they do, than I did two months ago. If it makes you feel any better, I've changed and it's because of you, okay? Now I just want to get Laura out of here and see what kind of lives we can rebuild somewhere. I'm sorry Sophie."

She leaned forward to kiss me, changed her mind and ran into the car. They drove off down Second Avenue.

It was all over now. It was over. I fumbled for a cigarette. I was out. It was time to quit anyway. It was really time to quit.

CHAPTER THIRTY-NINE

I stayed up typing the White Plains story for the *Feminist News* deadline. I worked straight through until the phone rang at nine in the morning. It was June Honeymoon.

"Well Susan, I wanted to be the first to tell you that you were wrong and I was right."

"Congratulations June, you're the first."

"Yes, they dropped your Grand Jury subpoena. Turns out the Westchester D.A. was involved in the whole affair. Transporting stolen goods et cetera. He's been under investigation for weeks. His assistant broke the story. A woman, Weinblatt or something like that, I thought that would make you happy. She wrote an expose about it for *New York Magazine* and now she owns the movie rights. It's very exciting. Anyway, so his word is worth ca-ca if you know what I mean and the police and FBI are suspending the investigation until that whole mess is cleared up. I have a few expenses, I'll send a messenger over with the bill. Don't forget to tip him. Bye."

I was sorry that she called because it made me sit still for a minute. It made me think about Vivian and Laura and miss not having them in my life anymore. Women. The world is full of these brilliant, beautiful, delicious women and all I want to do is love them and be good to them. But they're all so damaged. I could spend my life trying to put them back together again. And how about that Eva, I never said she wasn't smart. Now that she's rich, maybe she'll get rid of that jerk. You never know, maybe we could get together again someday. She was nice to me at Vivian's, maybe she still likes me. Maybe I should give her a call. I looked at the clock. "Oh shit." I had to get my copy over to the office before ten.

The collective took my copy to read over and discuss as I went across the street to Maude's for a glass of seltzer with lime and a plate of nachos. It was a good story, one of my best. Writing, it's like making love. First you dream about it and then one day it finally happens and it's nothing like you imagined. After a while it can be better than you ever thought or the absolute pits. Maybe I could really make it as a writer. The kind that goes on talk shows. I'd never have to really work, just write all the time and get invited to a lot of parties. I'd meet other writers and artists. Film-makers would ask me to do their screenplays. A bestseller, a TV series, I could write the first lesbian situation comedy. It would be great. I came into the office smiling.

"We're not running it." Chris looked at her shoes.

"Chrissie, every time I see you lately you're looking at your shoes. Did you just get a new pair or what?"

"Look Sophie, don't come down hard on me just because I'm the only one in this place who had the guts to tell you to your face. We're not printing it. It's a glorification of women who are male-identified. They embrace a male-left ideology and support violence as a strategy. You don't even criticize them. They're anti-feminist and besides the article is too long. We can't run it and that's all there is to say about it."

I threatened, I yelled and argued and bargained and cajoled. They were firm. I ran outside. It was the first snow of the year. It was falling. It was falling on me. Everyone in the street looked happy, remembering when they were kids, playing in the snow.

Sometimes I worry about what's going to happen to me. Sometimes I fantasize about the easy life, but really I don't expect it. I just want to enjoy things, have friends and keep my life interesting. If I stick to my instincts, the world will follow. I have to believe that. It was a cold day but I had two left gloves so I was warm. I lit a cigarette and walked off into the skyline.

A few of the publications of
THE NAIAD PRESS, INC.
P.O. Box 10543 • **Tallahassee, Florida 32302**
Mail orders welcome. Please include 15% postage.

The Sophie Horowitz Story by Sarah Schulman. A novel. 176 pp.
ISBN 0-930044-54-1 — $7.95

Amateur City by Katherine V. Forrest. A mystery novel. 224 pp.
ISBN 0-930044-55-X — $7.95

The Young in One Another's Arms by Jane Rule. A novel. 224 pp.
ISBN 0-930044-53-3 — $7.95

The Burnton Widows by Vicki P. McConnell. A mystery novel.
272 pp. ISBN 0-930044-52-5 — $7.95

Old Dyke Tales by Lee Lynch. Short Stories. 224 pp.
ISBN 0-930044-51-7 — $7.95

Daughters of a Coral Dawn by Katherine V. Forrest. Science
fiction. 240 pp. ISBN 0-930044-50-9 — $7.95

The Price of Salt by Claire Morgan. A novel. 288 pp.
ISBN 0-930044-49-5 — $7.95

Against the Season by Jane Rule. A novel. 224 pp.
ISBN 0-930044-48-7 — $7.95

Lovers in the Present Afternoon by Kathleen Fleming. A novel.
288 pp. ISBN 0-930044-46-0 — $8.50

Toothpick House by Lee Lynch. A novel. 264 pp.
ISBN 0-930044-45-2 — $7.95

Madame Aurora by Sarah Aldridge. A novel. 256 pp.
ISBN 0-930044-44-4 — $7.95

Curious Wine by Katherine V. Forrest. A novel. 176 pp.
ISBN 0-930044-43-6 — $7.50

Black Lesbian in White America. Short stories, essays,
autobiography. 144 pp. ISBN 0-930044-41-X — $7.50

Contract with the World by Jane Rule. A novel. 340 pp.
ISBN 0-930044-28-2 — $7.95

Yantras of Womanlove by Tee A. Corinne. Photographs.
64 pp. ISBN 0-930044-30-4 — $6.95

Mrs. Porter's Letter by Vicki P. McConnell. A mystery novel.
224 pp. ISBN 0-930044-29-0 — $6.95

To the Cleveland Station by Carol Anne Douglas. A novel.
192 pp. ISBN 0-930044-27-4 — $6.95

The Nesting Place by Sarah Aldridge. A novel. 224 pp.
ISBN 0-930044-26-6 — $6.95

This Is Not for You by Jane Rule. A novel. 284 pp.
ISBN 0-930044-25-8 — $7.95

Faultline by Sheila Ortiz Taylor. A novel. 140 pp.
ISBN 0-930044-24-X — $6.95

The Lesbian in Literature by Barbara Grier. 3d ed.
  Foreword by Maida Tilchen. A comprehensive bibliography.
  240 pp. ISBN 0-930044-23-1 $7.95

Anna's Country by Elizabeth Lang. A novel. 208 pp.
  ISBN 0-930044-19-3 $6.95

Prism by Valerie Taylor. A novel. 158 pp.
  ISBN 0-930044-18-5 $6.95

Black Lesbians: An Annotated Bibliography compiled by
  JR Roberts. Foreword by Barbara Smith. 112 pp.
  ISBN 0-930044-21-5 $5.95

The Marquise and the Novice by Victoria Ramstetter.
  A novel. 108 pp. ISBN 0-930044-16-9 $4.95

Labiaflowers by Tee A. Corinne. 40 pp.
  ISBN 0-930044-20-7 $3.95

Outlander by Jane Rule. Short stories, essays. 207 pp.
  ISBN 0-930044-17-7 $6.95

Sapphistry: The Book of Lesbian Sexuality by Pat Califia.
  2nd edition, revised. 195 pp. ISBN 0-930044-47-9 $7.95

The Black and White of It by Ann Allen Shockley.
  Short stories. 112 pp. ISBN 0-930044-15-0 $5.95

All True Lovers by Sarah Aldridge. A novel. 292 pp.
  ISBN 0-930044-10-X $6.95

A Woman Appeared to Me by Renee Vivien. Translated by
  Jeannette H. Foster. A novel. xxxi, 65 pp.
  ISBN 0-930044-06-1 $5.00

Cytherea's Breath by Sarah Aldridge. A novel. 240 pp.
  ISBN 0-930044-02-9 $6.95

Tottie by Sarah Aldridge. A novel. 181 pp.
  ISBN 0-930044-01-0 $5.95

The Latecomer by Sarah Aldridge. A novel. 107 pp.
  ISBN 0-930044-00-2 $5.00

VOLUTE BOOKS

Journey to Fulfillment	by Valerie Taylor	$3.95
A World without Men	by Valerie Taylor	$3.95
Return to Lesbos	by Valerie Taylor	$3.95
Desert of the Heart	by Jane Rule	$3.95
Odd Girl Out	by Ann Bannon	$3.95
I Am a Woman	by Ann Bannon	$3.95
Women in the Shadows	by Ann Bannon	$3.95
Journey to a Woman	by Ann Bannon	$3.95
Beebo Brinker	by Ann Bannon	$3.95

These are just a few of the many Naiad Press titles. Please request a
complete catalog!